Möllerke
Modern English for Mechanical Engineers

D1704203

Dieses Buch ist
Helmut Hildebrand (Linguist)
und Ursula Hildebrand (Bibliothekarin),
beide Dresden,
gewidmet.

Georg Möllerke

Modern English
for Mechanical Engineers

Ein kurzweiliges Trainingsbuch

Mit einer Audio-CD

Carl Hanser Verlag München Wien

El.-Ing. (grad.) Georg Möllerke
Engineering Report
CH-5415 Nussbaumen

Drawings by courtesy of
Bill Tidy, New Scientist, London
The Economist, London
Weltwoche, Zürich
Time Newsmagazine, New York
Newsweek, New York
U.S. News & World Report, New York

Die Deutsche Bibliothek CIP-Einheitsaufnahme

Modern English for Mechanical Engineers [Medienkombination] :
ein kurzweiliges Trainingsbuch ; mit einer Audio-CD / Georg
Möllerke. - München ; Wien : Hanser
    ISBN 3-446-21246-9
Audio-CD. 1999
Buch. 1999
    brosch.

Die Wiedergabe von Gebrauchsnamen, Handelsnamen, Warenbezeichnungen usw. in diesem
Werk berechtigt auch ohne besondere Kennzeichnung nicht zu der Annahme, daß solche Namen
im Sinne der Warenzeichen- und Markenschutz-Gesetzgebung als frei zu betrachten wären und
daher von jedermann benutzt werden dürften.

Dieses Werk ist urheberrechtlich geschützt.
Alle Rechte, auch die der Übersetzung, des Nachdrucks und der Vervielfältigung des Buches oder
Teilen daraus, vorbehalten. Kein Teil des Werkes darf ohne schriftliche Genehmigung des Verla-
ges in irgendeiner Form (Fotokopie, Mikrofilm oder ein anderes Verfahren), auch nicht für
Zwecke der Unterrichtsgestaltung, reproduziert oder unter Verwendung elektronischer Systeme
verarbeitet, vervielfältigt oder verbreitet werden.

© 1999 Carl Hanser Verlag München Wien
Internet: http://www.hanser.de
Umschlag: MCP • Agentur für Marketing - Communications - Production, Holzkirchen
Umbruch: WERKSATZ Schmidt & Schulz Gräfenhainichen
Druck und Bindung: Druckhaus „Thomas Müntzer" GmbH, Bad Langensalza
Printed in Germany

Vorwort

Das vorliegende Trainingsbuch ist für Studenten der Ingenieurwissenschaften, insbesondere des Maschinenbaues, sowie für Fachleute des Maschinen- und Anlagenbaues bestimmt, die ihre Englischkenntnisse erweitern wollen. Neben den reinen Fachtexten finden Sie auch reichlich kürzere Artikel aus dem Berufsleben, die von allgemeinem Interesse sind. Die Auflockerung mit Vignetten macht das Lesen vergnüglicher.

Dieses Buch ist gleichermaßen zum Englischlernen wie zur Erweiterung des Fachwissens gedacht. Der Leser erfährt von Trends in der Technik, ohne tiefschürfende Kenntnisse des Englischen besitzen zu müssen.

Neben den Originaltexten werden in der Randspalte die wichtigsten Begriffe in deutscher Sprache erläutert. Dem Leser bleibt somit das mühsame Nachschlagen in Wörterbüchern erspart; ganz abgesehen davon, dass viele Ausdrücke in Wörterbüchern gar nicht zu finden sind.

Die zum Buch gehörende Audio-CD bietet dem Leser eine wichtige Unterstützung. Es haben vier professionelle Sprecher mitgewirkt, unter ihnen der englische Schauspieler Ian Cummings; so hören Sie nicht nur korrektes Englisch, sondern auch angenehme Sprache.

Zu den Themen der Fachtexte gehören unter anderem: Dieselmotoren und Abgastechnik; Kraftwerke mit Hilfsbetrieben; Präzisionstechnik, Werkzeugmaschinen und Werkzeuge; Solartechnik; Brennstoffzellen in der Anwendung; Technik-Museen und Historisches.

Dieses Buch ist das einzige Trainingsbuch dieser Art für Ingenieurstudenten sowie Maschinen- und Anlagenbauer. Ich danke dem Carl Hanser Verlag München, insbesondere Herrn Jochen Horn, für die Unterstützung bei der Herausgabe und hoffe sehr, dass Sie viel Nutzen aus diesem Buch ziehen können.

CH-5415 Nussbaumen   *Georg Möllerke*

Inhaltsverzeichnis

Modern English for Mechanical Engineers on Audio-CD:

The conversion of cruise liner "Queen Elizabeth 2"

Six years ago, QE2 had been converted from a turbine ship into a vessel with a sophisticated engine-electric propulsion system.

It was to have been a festive day. The new liner "Queen Elizabeth 2" was embarking on its second "maiden voyage" after the £130 million overhaul that took her out of service for six months. But like the weather, the planned welcoming festivities fizzled.

Instead of a naval gun salute, a local high-school band welcomed the ship with 'Soul Man.'

New York's mayor was nearly an hour late. Worst of all, some 1,300 passengers complained that the voyage was not what it was touted to be. There were problems of flooding in some cabins, broken-down air conditioners in others, an inadequate telephone system and a health club that never opened.

In an effort to make amends, Cunard offered a reimbursement for all passengers, a total sum of about $1 million. "That refund will pay for our drinks bill," groused one disembarking man. Despite the grumblings, however, most of the passengers gave the ship high marks. Said one intrepid voyager: "If Cunard had canceled the crossing to iron out kinks, I suppose we would have all been very disappointed.

Electrical Review, London

conversion *hier:* Umbau; *sonst:* Umwandlung, Verwandlung
cruise liner Passagierschiff, Kreuzfahrtschiff
to convert umbauen, umwandeln, verwandeln
vessel Schiff; *sonst auch:* Gefäß, Behälter
sophisticated hochentwickelt, 'raffiniert'
engine *hier:* Dieselmotor
propulsion system Antriebsanlage
festive festlich, Fest...
to embark Passagiere und Fracht aufnehmen; *auch:* beginnen mit einem Vorhaben
maiden voyage Jungfernreise; **voyage** *allgemein:* längere Flug- oder Seereise
overhaul Überholung
festivities Festlichkeiten
to fizzle zum Misserfolg werden, danebengehen, schiefgehen
naval gun salute Salutschießen von Kriegsschiffen
mayor Bürgermeister
worst of all am allerschlimmsten
to complain sich beschweren
to tout ausrufen, verkünden
flooding Überfluten
inadequate unzureichend, ungenügend
effort Bemühen, Anstrengung
to make amends etwas gutmachen, kompensieren

reimbursement Entschädi-
   gung, Gutmachung, Rückvergütung
refund Rückzahlung
to grouse meckern, nörgeln
to disembark von Bord gehen,
   aussteigen
grumblings Murren, Schimpferei
high marks gute Noten
intrepid kühn, unerschrocken
to cancel streichen, absagen
crossing Überfahrt
to iron out ausbügeln
kinks *hier etwa:* Ungereimtheiten; *sonst:* Knoten, Verzerrungen

Sketch captions
bearing Lager
camshaft Nockenwelle
connecting rod Pleuelstange
crankcase Kurbelwanne
cylinder head Zylinderkopf
exhaust valve Auspuffventil
four-stroke engine Viertaktmotor
fuel injector Einspritzdüse
gudgeon pin Kolbenbolzen
piston Kolben
rated at mit einer Nenn-
   leistung von
rev/min revolutions per
   minute U/min
rocker arm Kipphebel
water cooling passage Kanal
   für Kühlwasserdurchlauf

Diesel engine, rated at 4800 kW, 500 rev/min

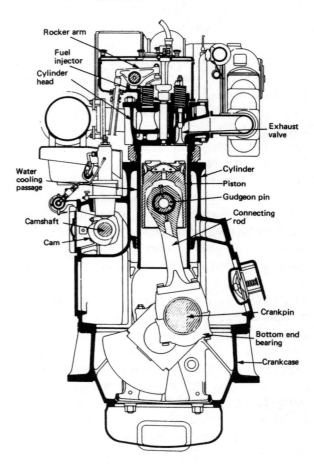

Four-stroke engine

Passenger ship 'Orania' at 25 knots

"Oriana" is the fastest cruise vessel now in service, sailing under the Red Ensign of P&O Cruises, London. Cruise speed is 25 knots.

She was delivered by the Meyer Werft of Papenburg in Germany and combines most advanced technology with the comfort and style of traditional ocean liners.

The length is 260 m and breadth 32 m. This ship is propelled by four non-reversible, four-stroke engines, with an output of $2 \times 11,900$ kW and $2 \times 7,900$ kW at 428 rpm. Each pair of engines transmits their power via a gearbox to a propeller shaft. Engine maker is MAN.

Four auxiliary diesel generator sets (MAN make), each rated at 4,420 kW, 514 rpm, provide the main electric power for this vessel. Further there are two shaft generators and an emergency generator set.

The Motor Ship, Sutton/Surrey, England

knots seamiles per hour; Knoten: 1,852 km/h
cruise vessel *auch:* cruise liner Kreuzfahrtschiff
red ensign rotes Zeichen; **ensign** *auch:* Flagge, (Rang-)Abzeichen
cruise speed Reisegeschwindigkeit, Marschfahrt
to deliver übergeben, abliefern
advanced hochentwickelt, fortgeschritten
to propel (an)treiben
non-reversible nicht umsteuerbar
four-stroke (diesel) engine Viertakt(diesel)motor
output abgegebene Leistung
rpm (or: rev/min) revolutions per minute
to transmit übertragen
gearbox Getriebe(kasten)
auxiliary diesel generator set Hilfs-D/G-Aggregat
each rated at jeder mit einer (Nenn-)Leistung von
to provide vorsehen, liefern
shaft Welle
emergency generator set Notstromaggregat

End of the line

end of the line Ende der Möglichkeiten, Ende der Leitung
to fold falten, umbiegen
fold Faltung
unable nicht in der Lage, unfähig
stack Stapel, Schichtung
to dwarf klein erscheinen lassen, in den Schatten stellen
from top to bottom von oben bis unten
to span umfassen, umspannen
growth Wachstum
to relegate zuschreiben; *sonst auch:* verbannen
realm Bereich, Fachgebiet; *auch:* Königreich
chip elektronischer Baustein, Plättchen
founder Gründer
to predict voraussagen
component Bauteil, Einzelteil, Komponente
to pack einbauen, einpacken
across *hier:* im Durchmesser

Take the largest, thinnest sheet of paper you can find. Fold it in half. Fold it in half again. After seven or eight folds, you will be unable to fold it by hand, as the sheet will have become as thick as a book. If 20 folds were possible, the stack of paper would dwarf your house. At 40 folds, it would be well on its way to the moon. Seventy folds would take it to the nearest star and on as far again, light would take eight years to go from top to bottom, and after 100 folds, it would be more than ten billion light years across and span the whole universe.

This is the essence of exponential growth: very small amounts rapidly become astronomically large through simply doubling.

So large in fact that exponential growth is relegated to the realm of mathematics, nothing in the real world can keep it up for long. For the past 30 years, though, chips have improved in a thoroughly exponential way.

Just as Gordon Moore, one of the founders of Intel, predicted, chips have been steadily doubling in power every two years. Engineers have, in effect, folded the paper 15 times, each time doubling the number of components they could pack on to a chip. Transistors on chips are now less than 0.5 millionths of a metre across.

Excerpt from The Economist, London

Such is accuracy

Precision engineering can now measure a shift in position of 0.0002 nanometres, or smooth a piece of quartz so that the rough peaks on its surface are no more than eight atoms tall. Such accuracy is bringing the mechanical engineer into a "realm where physics blends with chemistry", says Norman H. Brown of the Lawrence Livermore National Laboratory in the US.

Brown was speaking at a seminar on precision engineering, also known as "nanotechnology", at the Cranfield Institute of Technology last month. A nanometre is one-millionth of a millimetre; an atom is about 0.1 nanometres across. Nanotechnology's basic tools are diamond cutting edges that chip away pieces of material one micrometre across. Its products include optical parts for lasers, nozzles for ink-jet printers and components for computer memories.

Excerpt from The Economist, London

accuracy Genauigkeit, Präzision
precision engineering Präzisionstechnik
to measure messen
shift Verlagerung, Verschiebung
to smooth glätten
piece of quartz Quarzstück
rough grob, rauh
peak Spitze
surface Oberfläche
realm Bereich, Fachgebiet; *sonst:* Königreich
to blend sich verschmelzen, vermischen
across *hier:* im Durchmesser
cutting edge Schneidkante
to chip away abspanen, wegschneiden
nozzle Düse
ink-jet printer Tintenstrahldrucker
component Bauteil, Einzelteil

Keep an eye on the voltage level

If you use an accurate digital meter and check the mains voltage, you may well find it too high. Few people realise that even a small excess voltage can cut the life of a conventional tungsten lamp below the ususal 1000 hours, which are guaranteed.

There used to be a simple solution: Just buy bulbs rated for a higher voltage. But now that the whole of Britain's mains system is rated at 240 volts, the chances of finding a 250 volt bulb are slim.

The key factor is that the 240 volt rating is only the average. The electricity boards are free to let

to keep an eye on beachten, Augenmerk richten auf
voltage level Spannungsniveau
mains voltage Netzspannung
tungsten lamp Glühlampe; **tungsten** *sonst:* Wolfram
solution Lösung
bulb "Glühbirne," Glühlampe
rated at *hier:* mit einer Nennspannung von
slim gering, dürftig; *auch:* schlank

rating Bemessung, Auslegung
average Durchschnitt
electricity board Elektrizitätsbehörde
mean *hier:* Mittelwert
sub *hier:* Verteil..., Unter...
adequate ausreichend,
   genügend
to push out *hier:* unterdrücken
to cope with fertigwerden mit
fluctuation Schwankung
to cause verursachen, bewirken
peak (*or:* **top**) **demand**
   Höchstbedarf, Spitzenbedarf
slack schwach; *sonst auch:*
   schlaff, locker
period Zeitraum, Periode

the mains wander up or down by six per cent. That is a swing of 29 volts; more than the 14 volts above or below the 240 volt mean. Some homes will run above the 240 volt line and others below it. It depends on the length of underground cables between the home and the nearest transformer substation. The longer the the cable run, the higher its resistance and the lower the voltage. To give distant homes adequate voltage, the sub-station has to push out a voltage which is above the mean. So homes close to the substation are likely to be well over the 240 volt level.

The electricity boards have also to cope with fluc-tuations of load, caused by weather changes, and peak or slack periods of demand.

Excerpt from New Scientist, London

Fuel cell engine ready for the industry

fuel cell Brennstoffzelle;
   Stromquelle, in der durch
   elektrochemische Oxidation
   von Brennstoff mit Sauerstoff chemische Energie
   direkt in elektrische Energie
   umgewandelt wird
engine Motor; *sonst auch:*
   Triebwerk
barrister Anwalt
to invent erfinden
transition Übergang, Durchgang
to announce ankündigen, verkünden
energy source Energiequelle
to emit abgeben, ausstrahlen,
   emittieren

Sir William Grove, a famous barrister, invented the fuel cell in 1839, but only now has it made the transition from 19th-century curiosity to the ulti-mate in clean-car technology.

The Canadian company Ballard Power Systems announced last month that this silent energy source, which emits only water vapour, has achieved the power density – power per weight and volume – required for use in a car.

The claim was made at the International Grove Fuel Cell Conference in London. Ballard, based in Vancouver, developed the cell under a joint programme with Daimler-Benz.

According to Mr. Firoz Rasul, Ballard's chief executive, the US Department of Energy had estimated that a fuel-cell engine should eventually cost about the same as an internal combustion engine of the same volume.

Sir William's invention exploits the energy given off by the chemical reactions of burning, in this case the burning that results from the strong affinity of oxygen for hydrogen.

However, in the fuel cell the energy comes out as electricity, not fire, because the electrons that pass from one element to another in the reaction are harnessed by an external circuit.

With few moving parts, the fuel cell is quiet and demands little maintenance. The new cell is capable of producing 1,000 watts per litre and 700 watts per kilogram, or over 28 kilowatts per cubic foot.

The Weekly Telegraph, London

water vapour Wasserdampf
to achieve erreichen
power density Leistungsdichte
weight Gewicht
required erforderlich, nötig
claim Bekanntgabe; *auch:*
  Behauptung, Anspruch
to develop entwickeln
joint gemeinsam
chief executive *etwa:* Generaldirektor
to estimate schätzen, vermuten
eventual(ly) schließlich,
  letzten Endes
internal combustion engine
  Verbrennungskraftmaschine
to exploit nutzen, ausbeuten
to result from sich ergeben
  aus, resultieren aus
oxygen Sauerstoff
hydrogen Wasserstoff
to harness nutzen, einspannen
external circuit Außenkreis,
  äußerer Stromkreis
to demand fordern, verlangen
maintenance Wartung,
  Instandhaltung

Significant reduction of engine exhausts

Inspired by physics of the upper atmosphere, a group of German researchers has devised a way to cut dramatically the toxic emissions of nitrogen oxides and sulphur dioxide from diesel engines. Their experimental system pumps an electric current through the exhaust gases to render the pollutants harmless.

In Britain, diesel engines present a growing pollution hazard as the number of cars with diesel

significant bedeutsam, wichtig
engine exhausts *hier:* Abgase
  von Dieselmotoren
to devise sich ersinnen, ausdenken
to cut *hier:* verringern
toxic giftig, Schadstoff...
nitrogen Stickstoff
sulphur Schwefel...
current Strom

to render es schaffen, machen
pollutants Schadstoffe, Verunreinigungen
to present darstellen
hazard Gefahr
to increase sich erhöhen, anwachsen
carbon Kohlenstoff...
petrol-burning mit Benzin arbeitend; *wörtlich:* Benzin verbrennend
to generate erzeugen
to develop entwickeln
catalytic converter Katalysator
to fit einbauen, montieren, einsetzen, vorsehen
shower of sparks Funkenregen
oxygen Sauerstoff
lean-burn petrol engine Benzin-"Magermotor"

engines on the road continues to increase. According to the Society of Motor Traders and Manufacturers, 22.5 per cent of all new cars last year were powered by diesel engines.

Diesel vehicles produce less carbon monoxide and carbon dioxide than their petrol-burning equivalents, but they generate larger amounts of nitrogen oxides and sulphur dioxide.

The German system for reducing pollutants is being developed by Klaus Pochner and co-workers at the Fraunhofer Institute for Laser Technology in Aachen. Instead of trying to build a catalytic converter, they fitted electrodes into the engine's exhaust system. A current passes between the electrodes, producing a shower of sparks which ionise the exhaust gases to produce nitrogen, oxygen and sulphur.

"You can remove 95 per cent of nitrogen oxides if you use enough energy," says Pochner, "and this system will also work on lean-burn petrol engines."

Excerpt from New Scientist, London

Increasing demand for cruise vessels

increasing ansteigend, wachsend
demand Nachfrage, Bedarf, Forderung
cruise vessel Kreuzfahrtschiff
commonplace alltäglich
efficient leistungsfähig, effektiv
crammed vollgestopft, dichtgedrängt
cruising event Ereignis bei einer Kreuzfahrt
maiden voyage Jungfernreise

Huge 70,000-tonners carrying far more than 2,000 passengers are becoming commonplace. Traditional are they not; some look more like Miami Beach apartment blocks than the ships of yesterday. But they are comfortable, efficient and crammed with high technology.

One of the latest cruising events was the maiden voyage of P & O's 67,000-ton 'Oriana'. A dozen or so new megaships over the 50,000-ton mark will enter service in the next two years, costing a couple of hundred million sterling apiece, and carrying anything from a thousand to two thousand passengers.

Older vessels like Cunard's 'Queen Elizabeth 2' and P&O's 'Canberra' still enjoy megastar status. Many aging Clyde-built veterans are still earning their keep as cruise liners, making up for the lack of youth with their reassuring brass-and-teak charm. Even the gigantic liner 'United States' may return to the cruise circuit after a quarter of a century in mothballs.

There are jazz cruises, bridge-playing cruises and photography cruises. There are also Polar cruises on Russian icebreakers. And there are hairy-chested adventure cruises where dressing for dinner means duffel coats and seaboots.

Somewhere in the middle of all this niche marketing are the great majority of cruises, aimed at the huge middle-class, middle-income market of cruise passengers from a score of nations.

Excerpt from High Life, British Airways

to enjoy sich erfreuen
to earn the keep sein Geld verdienen
to make up for wettmachen, ausgleichen
lack of youth das Fehlen des Neuen (*oder:* der Jugend)
reassuring beruhigend
brass-and-teak aus Messing und Teakholz bestehend
cruise circuit Kreuzfahrtroute; **circuit** *auch für:* Stromkreis, Wasserkreis, Kreislauf
mothball Mottenkugel
hairy-chested halsbrecherisch, waghalsig, riskant
aimed at abzielend auf, absehend auf
score Menge, enorme Zahl

Market for well-maintained engines

Fumes from diesel engines may well cause cancer, as the Royal Commission pointed out this autumn. But the concern is not new. "Throughout 1955 and the early part of 1956 there was a recurring suggestion that exhaust gas from diesel engines was an important factor to lung cancer," said London Transport's annual report for 1956.

Local authorities in London were so worried about it that they pressed London Transport to keep its electric trolleybuses and not to replace them with diesel-engined polluters.

However: "Investigations by Research Council's group for research on atmospheric pollution, in

well-maintained gut erhalten und gepflegt
engine (Diesel-)Motor
fume unangenehmer Rauch, Dampf
to cause verursachen, bewirken
to point out darauf hinweisen, feststellen
concern Besorgnis, Sorge
recurring wiederkehrend, immer wieder auftretend
suggestion Meinung; *sonst auch:* Vorschlag
exhaust gas Abgas(e)

annual jährlich, Jahres …
authority Verwaltung, Behörde
to replace ersetzen
polluter (Umwelt-)Verschmutzer, Umweltverseucher
investigation Untersuchung
research council Forschungsrat, Forschungskomitee
pollution *hier:* Umweltverschmutzung
to confirm bestätigen, bekräftigen
to constitute bilden, darstellen
upshot Fazit, Endergebnis
fortuitous zufällig

which London Transport willingly cooperated, confirmed that the exhaust from a well-maintained diesel engine constitutes no danger to health."
The upshot of this fortuitous research result was that, take a deep breath, London Transport ordered 850 diesel-engined buses to replace the trolleybuses.
New Scientist, London

IEEE recommendations for engineers

recommendation Empfehlung
advice Rat(schlag)
to behave sich verhalten
casual nicht auffällig, salopp, sportlich
to avoid vermeiden
to wear tragen
to advertise affluence Wohlhabenheit zur Schau stellen
affiliation Zugehörigkeit
to attend beiwohnen, teilhaben, besuchen
work-related die Arbeit betreffend, zur Arbeit gehörend
identification badge Abzeichen (*oder:* Schild) zur Identifikation, Zeichen zur Erkennung
corporate betreffend eines Unternehmens
to disclose preisgeben, aufdecken

The American Institute of Electronic and Electrical Engineers, New York, published a newsletter to their members giving advice how to behave abroad.
– Dress in conservative, casual clothes in order to avoid calling attention to yourself.
– Don't wear expensive jewelry, furs, etc., carry expensive cameras or otherwise advertise affluence.
– Don't wear clothing or jewelry advertising your U.S. affiliation or religion. Don't carry religious or political books, magazines or cards.
– Don't tell strangers the name of your company or what business you're in. If attending a work-related meeting, don't wear identification badges in public. If you must bring corporate or government ID on your trip, carry it in your checked baggage.
– Don't disclose your itinerary or hotel plans to strangers, but make sure that someone you trust is advised of your daily travel plans.
– Obtain maps and detailed directions for your destinations. Avoid getting lost. Upon arrival in a

city, locate the nearest police station and American consulate or embassy.
– Stay alert and sober at all times.
– Allow plenty of time (at least two hours) for security checks for international flights, both at home and abroad. Be prepared for intense security measures, also answering questions, filling out forms, having your luggage searched and being frisked.
– Don't linger in crowded public access areas. Go directly to your airline's baggage and passenger check-in counter, clear security and wait near the departure gate. People in the boarding areas have already passed through security checkpoints.
– Never make wisecracks in the vicinity of security checkpoints.
IEEE Newsletter, New York

itinerary Reiseziel
to trust vertrauen
to advise unterrichten, mitteilen; *sonst auch:* (an)raten
to obtain sich beschaffen, erhalten
destination Zielort
to get lost Orientierung verlieren, sich verlaufen
to locate *hier:* den Sitz feststellen, lokalisieren
embassy Botschaft
to stay alert wachsam bleiben, auf der Hut sein
sober nüchtern
measure *hier:* Vorkehrung
to be frisked durchsucht werden, 'gefilzt' werden
to linger verweilen, zurückbleiben
public access area Räumlichkeit(en) für öffentlichen Zugang
wisecracks schlaue Bemerkungen, Witzeleien
vicinity Nähe

Food for thought

Every time we run a joke in this column, readers write in to tell us they've heard it before. So let's just hope that at least some of you haven't already come across this little gem, which is doing the rounds of the engineering discussion groups on the Net. – Two undergrade engineers at Newcastle University did very well in their mid-term exams. Their practical results were squeaky clean, both were heading for a first. In fact, the two friends were so certain of their chances that they spent the weekend before finals fellwalking and partying at a hilltop youth hostel.

food for thought das gibt (aber) zu denken
column Kolumne, Spalte
to come across *etwa:* bekannt vorkommen, schon einmal begegnet sein
gem Prachtstück, Edelstein
mid-term Zwischen ..., *sonst auch:* mittelfristig
result Ergebnis, Resultat
squeaky clean *hier etwa:* astrein

to head for a first an die Spitze gelangen, erste(r) sein
fell-walking Bergwandern; **fell** *auch:* Hügel
youth hostel Jugendherberge
crucial entscheidend, wichtig
final Schluss …, End …
flat tyre *hier:* einen 'Platten'
spare *hier:* Reservereifen
dud *hier:* platt; *sonst:* Reinfall
lenient nachsichtig, milde
relieved erleichtert, entspannt
voltage behaviour Spannungsverhalten
squirrel-cage induction motor Käfigläufermotor
unprepared unvorbereitet
tyre (US: **tire**) Autoreifen

Either because of all the fresh air or a few too many beers on the Sunday night, they didn't make it back to Newcastle until mid-Monday morning, by which time the crucial final exam already had started. Instead of going in late, they spoke to their professor and explained that their car got a flat tyre on the way back to university and the spare was dud. The professor was a lenient chap and agreed they could take the exam the following day.

The friends were extremely relieved and studied hard that night. Come the exam, they were put in separate rooms and given the paper. Question one was simple: Voltage behaviour when starting squirrel cage induction motors (five points). So the students thought the exam was going to be easy. They were unprepared, however, for what they saw on the next page. It said: "Which tyre? (95 points)."
Feedback in New Scientist, London

Spelling it out

to spell out (mühsam) entziffern; *auch:* darlegen
to suggest vorschlagen
subtitled mit Untertiteln versehen
responsible *hier:* ist zuzuschreiben; *sonst:* verantwortlich sein
proficiency Tüchtigkeit, Können
to exploit nutzen; *sonst auch:* ausbeuten
phenomenon Phänomen
literacy Fähigkeit zu lesen und zu schreiben
legislation Gesetzgebung
subtitle Untertitel
dubbing Synchronisieren
command *hier:* Beherrschen

It has been suggested that subtitled films are responsible for Swedes' proficiency in English (Letters, 2 August, p 49). How about exploiting this phenomenon to improve literacy within the English-speaking world – especially in Britain.

Legislation to add English subtitles to all films, including those already in English, and to ban all dubbing, could be a cheap way of improving British people's command of languages – including their own.
David Bailey, Cambridge; in New Scientist

William Shockley, famous inventor

William Shockley, who died nine years ago, was fairly described as having revolutionised our lives by his leading role in the development of the transistor. But he was a prickly fellow, especially when riding the hobby horse he mounted after his transistor days, that of maintaining that black people are genetically inferior to whites.

On one London visit he was asked to be the guest of the Association of British Science Writers for a lunch and agreed to appear. The custom of the functions is that the distinguished guest answers questions from the journalists who make up the rest of the party.

William Shockley became heated almost immediately when the black and white subject arose, demanding to know what gave anyone the right to ask him anything and refusing to answer on the grounds that the questioner was not qualified to receive information. Coming from someone who had accepted the invitation and the terms of it, I thought this a bit rich.

New Scientist, London

inventor Erfinder
was fairly described wurde gerechterweise (*auch: gerecht, richtig*) dargestellt *oder:* beschrieben
leading role führende Rolle
development Entwicklung
prickly schwierig; *sonst auch:* dornig, stechend, stachelig
to mount sich widmen, besteigen
to maintain behaupten; *sonst auch:* beibehalten
inferior minderwertig, zweitklassig
to appear erscheinen
custom Brauch, Gewohnheit
distinguished geehrt, verdient
he became heated er regte sich auf
subject Thema, Gegenstand
to demand fordern, verlangen
to refuse sich weigern, verweigern
terms Voraussetzungen, Bedingungen

Silent witness

Spies, the police and reporters who want to record a conversation clandestinely will find a new tapeless recorder a boon. The Retell, which costs around £120, uses solid-state memory instead of tape and records up to 60 minutes. Smaller than a cigarette packet and with no moving parts, it is

witness Zeuge, Zeugnisaussage
spy Spion
clandestine(ly) heimlich, versteckt
tapeless ohne Band

boon Segen, Wohltat, Gefälligkeit
solid-state memory Festkörperspeicher
to record aufnehmen, aufzeichnen
moving parts bewegliche Teile
to connect anschließen,
schalten
telltale clicks verräterisches
Klicken

completely silent. It can also be connected to a
phone without making those telltale clicks typical
for tapes.
(New Scientist, London)

Silicon Valley reveals Tech museum

to unveil eröffnen, enthüllen
era Ära, Zeitabschnitt
innovation Erneuerung, Erfindung
shrine Heiligtum, Schrein
exterior das Äußere
to devote weihen, widmen
chat room "Treff-"Lokal,
Raum für Plaudereien
space travel Raumfahrt
minds on was das (ganze)
Denken beeinflußt
to bolster stärken; *sonst auch:*
künstlich aufrecht erhalten
to design konstruieren, entwerfen
roller caster Achterbahnwagen
to join verbinden, verflechten,
zusammenfügen
baby boomers Menschen aus
starken Geburtsjahrgängen
to stand apart für sich (selbst)
betrachten
to draw anziehen

Sooner or later every era gets a monument of its
own. Now comes the Museum of Innovation,
called Tech, Silicon Valley's $ 96 million shrine to
itself.
Twenty years in the making, the museum with the
mango orange exterior opens this year in downtown San Jose. Devoted to technology in all of its
manifestations – from chat rooms of the Internet
to space travel – the museum specializes in what
it calls "minds on" exhibits that go far beyond
simple interactivity.
In the Innovation Gallery, for instance, you can
bolster your intelligence by designing a roller-
coaster ride that you can then program into the
Cyclone – a real two-seater coaster car. A digital
studio lets you star in a film. Known simply as
the Tech, the museum joins centers of science and
technology that have grown in recent years as
baby boomers clamor for more ways to put their
kids in touch with their inner Bill Gates.
But if the Tech stands apart, it is for its one-of-a-
kind exhibits that demonstrate the same high level
of innovation that made Silicon Valley what it is.

The Tech is expected to draw more than 650,000 visitors a year to this Californian town.
Excerpt from Newsweek, New York

Engine fuel in Europe and America

After the war one could have seen many U.S. trucks on the roads in Germany driven by petrol engines. I remember well how quiet those Studebaker trucks were; the same type of vehicle America had been delivering to the Soviet Union during the war.

Probably the petrol consumption of those 5.5-tonners was forty litres per hundred kilometres; even Jeeps consumed more than thirty litres. If those Studebakers had been equipped with diesel engines, the fuel consumption might have been below 25 litres.

However, that was another time, petrol was cheap in the USA. When buying a car, low fuel consumption was not a decisive factor. But in the seventies there was a change in economy with regard to consumption of mineral oil.

Nowadays, one scarcely finds delivery vans not driven by diesel engines. Also ship's propulsion has undergone a radical change. It is now ten years since the last turbine ship was built for an American shipping company. Since then no merchant vessels have gone into service not fitted with diesel engines.

The highest output of low-speed diesel engines for ship's propulsion is now 60 000 kW at only 100 rev/min. Exclusively heavy oil is being provided for marine diesel engines. All this raises the question: If the fuel consumption is so low, why aren't all motor-cars fitted with diesel engines?

engine fuel Treibstoff für Motoren; *hier gemeint:* Otto- und Dieselmotoren
truck *(US)* Last(kraft)wagen; *GB:* lorry
petrol engine Ottomotor
quiet ruhig(laufend)
vehicle Fahrzeug
to deliver liefern, übergeben
probable (-bly) wahrscheinlich
petrol consumption Benzinverbrauch
jeep geländegängiges Fahrzeug, entstanden aus General-Purpose Vehicle
to consume verbrauchen
to equip versehen, ausrüsten
decisive entscheidend
economy Wirtschaftlichkeit
with regard to hinsichtlich
scarce(ly) (sehr) selten
delivery van Lieferwagen
ship's propulsion Schiffsantrieb
shipping company Reederei
merchant vessel Handelsschiff
to go *(or:* put) **into service** in Dienst stellen
to fit versehen, ausrüsten
output (abgegebene) Leistung
low-speed langsamlaufend
exclusive(ly) ausschließlich
heavy oil Schweröl

to provide vorsehen, liefern
marine diesel engine Schiffsdieselmotor
to raise the question die Frage
  erheben
to explain erklären, erläutern
pure rein, nur
economical wirtschaftlich
consideration Betrachtung,
  Überlegung
current momentan, jetzig
to suffer a collaps einen
  Kollaps erleiden
crack plant Crackanlage,
  'Spaltanlage'
to establish errichten, aufbauen
financial means Finanzmittel
wave of unemployment Welle
  der Arbeitslosigkeit
to sweep hindurchfegen
sulphur content Schwefelgehalt
disadvantage Nachteil
toxic giftig, mit Schadstoffen
  versehen
exhaust gas Abgas(e)
to decide (sich) entscheiden
to reduce verringern, reduzieren
considerable (-bly) beträchtlich
to lower herabsetzen
proposal Plan, Vorschlag
interim solution Zwischenlösung
to turn down ablehnen
to be in for gut sein für,
  erstaunt sein über
surprise Überraschung
available zu haben, verfügbar

The answer is: It is not possible with regard to the world economy. This might be explained by pure economical considerations. If a large mineral company only sells 60 per cent of its current oil sales, it would suffer a collaps, very soon. Also think of the huge crack plants established with enormous financial means, a wave of unemployment would sweep many countries.

But how about the sulphur content? One of the disadvantages of diesel oil are toxic exhaust gases. Fifteen ministers at a Luxembourg meeting decided: The sulphur content must be reduced considerably. Currently, the sulphur in diesel oil is more than 350 ppm (parts per million). By 2005 the content shall be lowered to 50 ppm. The proposal for an interim solution of 100 ppm by 2000 was turned down by the ministers. But we may be in for a surprise: In Sweden and Switzerland diesel oil with low-content sulphur has now been available for more than three years. However, the refinery works are in Germany.

Georg Möllerke, Engineering Report

The electronic weatherman at home

Oregon Scientific Inc., a company based in Portland, Oregon, is marketing an electronic barometer that constantly displays the local forecast. Called the Home Weather Forecaster, it features a four-line liquid-crystal screen that uses easy-to-understand symbols to indicate future weather changes: sunny, partly sunny, cloudy, rainy and stormy. "It's like having a 24-hour weather person at home," says David Childers, vice president of sales and marketing. "You'll never have to adjust your schedule around TV or radio weather programs because the device provides to-the-minute predicitons." The unit measures rising or falling barometric pressure within a 25-miles area. Forecasts are 75 percent accurate from 12 to 24 hours in advance, says the maker. If a hard rain is about to fall, a storm icon appears on the screen and, just to make sure you're alerted, the device emits a beep until the weather improves. The barometer can be silenced by pressing any of its buttons. Other features include indoor and outdoor temperature – in either Fahrenheit or Celsius – and a calendar/alarm clock. The unit, which measures 7 inches by 1 inch by 4 inches, runs on four AAA batteries. It has a built-in stand for tabletop use; it can also be hung on a wall. The Home Weather Forecaster takes approximately 24 hours to acclimate itself to a next location. Cost: $ 90 in America.

U.S. News & World Report, New York

weatherman Meteorologe
based in mit Hauptsitz in
forecast Voraussage
to feature als Besonderheit aufweisen
liquid-crystal screen Bildschirm mit Flüssigkristall-Anzeige
to indicate anzeigen; *sonst auch:* kennzeichnen
to adjust angleichen, justieren
schedule Plan, Tabelle
to provide vorsehen, liefern
prediction Vorhersage, Prognose
to measure messen, angeben
accurate genau, präzise
in advance im voraus
icon Zeichen; *sonst auch:* Ikone, Heiligenbild
alerted auf der Hut, alarmiert; *sonst auch:* aufgeweckt
device Gerät, Apparatur
to press a button einen Knopf drücken
to measure Abmessungen aufweisen
built-in eingebaut
for tabletop use auf den Tisch zu stellen
to acclimate sich akklimatisieren, gewöhnen an

History for yoo-hoo

to catch on Anklang finden, einschlagen; *sonst auch:* 'kapieren'

urgent dringend, dringlich, eilig

message Meldung

to communicate mitteilen, übertragen

servant Diener

to prove sich erweisen

call office Fernsprechbüro

lavatory Toilette

attendant Aufseher

to perform ausführen, vornehmen

to put a call through einen Anruf durchstellen

operator 'Fräulein vom Amt'

environmental impact *etwa:* Einfluß des Umweltgedankens; **impact** *auch:* Aufprall, Einschlag, Wirkung

rural areas ländliche Gebiete

thatched roof Strohdach

logs Holzblöcke

gazebo Gebäude mit schönem Ausblick, Aussichtspunkt

spacious geräumig

to remove entfernen, herausnehmen

to discover entdecken

When the telephone system started in the 1870s, the Post Offfice was not very enthusiastic. They thought it would be too expensive ever to catch on, and that anyway if you had an urgent message to communicate, then your servant could always carry it for you. Nevertheless, the system proved popular enough for the first public "call offices" to be introduced in 1884.

With some of the early telephone boxes you had to put a penny in the slot to open the door, as with a public lavatory. Others had attendants who took your money and performed the complicated business of putting a call through to the operator for you.

With an eye to what would now be called "environmental impact," some boxes in rural areas had thatched roofs, and were made of logs in the manner of an Edwardian gazebo. They were spacious, too, with table and chairs. These were removed after a policeman discovered four men inside one, having a smoke and playing cards on a Sunday.

"Feedback" in New Scientist, London

"Have a look at the mileage and you'll know you've made a bargain."

A major engineering achievement: Pioneer 10

Lost in space. The last signals from Pioneer 10 to Earth took nearly ten hours – but some time ago, this spacecraft fell silent.

When Pioneer 10 vaulted into the sky in 1972, its predicted life span was 21 months – enough for it to fulfill its stated mission of reaching Jupiter. The spacecraft didn't quit there. For the past 26 years, the craft has flown the solar system, beaming data to Earth. But its scientific value has dwindled. Scientists finally switched off the Earth-based sensors that received its signals.

It was the first spacecraft to reach Jupiter; the first to travel through the fearsome asteroid belt between Mars and Jupiter; the first to leave the solar system. Thanks to Pioneer 10, scientists learned that Jupiter is a liquid planet and that the solar wind, charged particles from the sun, can be felt far beyond the orbits of the outermost planets.

Pioneer 10 is now over 7 billion miles from the sun. It will continue to coast through deep space but no one on this planet will ever get word of the craft's journey. The only possible observers now are extraterrestrials smart enough to read a plaque on the spacecraft. Designed by Carl Sagan and others, it shows a man, a woman, and a map to Earth.

New Scientist, London

major bedeutend; *auch:* wichtig
achievement Leistung, Errungenschaft
space *hier:* Weltraum, Weltall
to vault *hier:* sich erheben, schwingen; *sonst auch:* springen
to predict voraussagen
stated *hier:* bestimmt
to quit aufgeben, verlassen
craft Raumfahrzeug
to beam abgeben, strahlen
value Wert, Bedeutung
to dwindle nachlassen, dahinschwinden
to receive empfangen, erhalten
to share teilen
explorer Entdecker
fearsome gefahrvoll; *sonst auch:* schrecklich, grausam
belt Gürtel
charged aufgeladen
orbit Umlaufbahn
plaque Gedenktafel; *sonst auch:* Namensschild

Reinventing the diesel engine

to reinvent neu erfinden	
diesel engine Dieselmotor; *im Englischen nicht:* 'diesel motor'	
to stake a claim Anspruch anmelden, Anspruch erheben	
environmentally friendly umweltfreundlich	
medium-term thinking mittelfristiges Denken	
fuel Treibstoff, Brennstoff	
they vied with each other (to vie) sie wetteiferten untereinander	
to bill verkünden (zum Beispiel durch Plakate)	
to refer to sich beziehen auf	
meagre kärglich, dürftig, mager, dürr	
capable imstande, fähig	
direct injection Direkteinspritzung	
is hitting the road ist auf der Straße anzutreffen; *oder:* zu finden	
engine option Auswahl des Motors	
turn of events Änderung der Gegebenheiten; **event** *auch:* Ereignis, Vorfall	
controlled gesteuert	
smooth weich, glatt	
petrol Benzin; *US:* gasoline	
filthy unangenehm, schmutzig	

Strange as it may seem, diesel oil is staking a claim to be the environmentally fuel in the car makers' medium-term thinking. For car makers, at least, smaller certainly seems more beautiful. At the recent Paris Motor Show they vied with each other to show small, economical cars, such as the tiny Volkswagen Lupo and the Toyota Yaris.

The Lupo is billed as the world's first 3-litre car – the number referring not to the size of its engine, but to its meagre thirst. It's the first car capable of travelling 100 kilometres on three litres of fuel, or about 90 miles to the gallon.

What makes this possible is a new kind of TDI diesel engine, turbo-charged with dirct injection. The same technology, which has already appeared in a new BMW, is also hitting the road in a Mercedes, an Alfa Romeo, and in cars from Peugeot, Rover and Volkwagen. Soon it will be common to all manufacturers' models as an engine option. Suddenly, diesel is cool.

Behind this unlikely turn of events is a newer generation of electronically controlled, high pressure fuel-injection systems combined with new "common-rail" technology. This promises to make diesel as quiet and smooth as petrol, while offering much greater fuel economy. It is also cleaner. After years as the poor, filthy relation to petrol engines, diesel has cleaned itself up.

Excerpt from The Economist, London

Worldwatch Institute reports on means of transport

Why are cars the preferred form of urban personal transport? Riding a bicycle will save you money, create less pollution, make you healthier and let you zip past heavy traffic. Will anything persuade auto owners to hop on a two-wheeler?

Absolutely yes, says a report from Washington's Worldwatch Institute.

In "Taking bikes seriously," senior researcher Gary Gardner shows how cities around the world have increased bike ridership by offering little encouragement. The city of Copenhagen, for example, makes 2,300 bicycles available for public use; the $ 3 rental fee is refunded when the bike is returned.

In Lima, Peru, low-income residents can buy bicycles through a special small-loan program. During the 1980s Japan helped bikers by boosting the number of bicycle parking spaces at railway stations about fourfold, to 2.4 million. That strategy saved both money and land; two bikes can fit into a square meter of parking space.

The Worldwatch report also notes the growing use of bicycles among police forces worldwide. More than 2,000 police departments now use two-wheelers, and a survey found that arrest rates often jumped after bike controls were introduced. "The secret to this effectiveness is stealth," says Worldwatch's Gardner. "A bike cop sees more, and is less seen, than a colleague in a car – and the bike is better for the environment."

Wendy Kan; U.S. News & World Report

to report berichten
means of transport Transportmittel
preferred bevorzugt
urban personal transport Personen-Stadttransport
to create schaffen, kreieren
pollution Umweltverschmutzung
to zip *hier:* überholen; *sonst:* schwirren, rauschen
to persuade überreden, zureden
two-wheeler Zweirad
serious(ly) ernst(haft)
senior älterer, Chef …
to increase erhöhen, zunehmen, vergrößern
bike ridership Gemeinschaft der Radfahrer
to offer bieten
encouragement Ermutigung
available verfügbar, zu haben
rental fee Miet-, Leihgebühr
to refund zurückerstatten, rückvergüten, gutmachen
resident Bewohner
small-loan Kleinkredit
to boost erhöhen, steigern
to fit into hineinpassen in
to note feststellen, bemerken
survey Nachforschung, Überprüfung
arrest rates Anzahl der Festnahmen
to introduce einführen

effectiveness Wirkung;
  auch: Leistungsvermögen,
  Effektivität
stealth *hier:* Unauffälligkeit;
  sonst: Heimlichkeit
environment Umwelt

Slim and willowy

slim and willowy rank und
  schlank
to advertise anpreisen, propagieren
to lose weight Gewicht abnehmen
to inspire inspirieren, veranlassen
to toss (hinüber)schieben,
  werfen
the letter inside read im Brief
  stand geschrieben
to invite cordially herzlich
  einladen
class reunion Klassentreffen,
  -zusammenkunft; **reunion**
  auch: Versöhnung, Wieder-
  vereinigung

A friend of mine had tried every diet advertised with no success. But suddenly he started losing weight.
Asking him what new program had inspired him he tossed me an envelope to open. The letter read: "You are cordially invited to your 20th class reunion."
Walter Cogdell, Washington Post

... the designer must have an adequate knowledge of manufacturing, repairability, instrumentation and cost estimating.

Language barrier

language barrier Sprachbarriere, -schranke
to remark on sich äußern,
  bemerken über
by the time *hier:* bis er soweit
  ist
to cross the Channel den
  Kanal überqueren

A Dorset schoolmaster remarked on one of his pupils: "By the time that boy learns French, he will be too old to cross the Channel."
From The Week, London

Theatrical air

A man called on Sir John Gielgud in his theatre dressing room to congratulate him on his performance.
Sir John said, "How pleased I am to meet you. I
used to know your son – we were at school
together."
The man replied, "I have no son. At school I was
with you."
The Week, London

to call on besuchen
theatre dressing room
   Theatergarderobe
performance *hier:* Darstellung auf der Bühne; *sonst:*
   Leistung
I used to know ich kannte,
   ich pflegte zu kennen

Fairgrounds yield high rewards

Roam around Germany and you might get the impression that the national speciality is not some industry such as cars or machine tools, but trade fairs.
Every biggish city boasts its exhibtion centre
(Messe); and local economies often move to the
rhythm of big fairs. Now trades are building new
halls and modernising old ones.
Business certainly seems to be booming. Last
year German trade fairs attracted record numbers
and visitors, partly because several big fairs coin-
cided. Exhibition centres had revenues of DM 3.2
billion ($ 2.2 billion) and generated another
DM 11 billion or so in business of hotels, taxis,
restaurants and shops in host cities.
Trade fairs are the only industry where German
dominance looks safe. Germany has three of the
world's five biggest fairgrounds and claims to host
two-thirds of the 150 leading international affairs.
Berlin's biennial Funkausstellung bills itself as
the world's biggest consumer-electronics show
for the general public. Part of the secret of the
success is that fairgrounds are owned by cities
and state governments.

fairground Messegelände
to yield einbringen, ergeben;
   sonst auch: ernten
reward(s) Gewinn; *sonst auch:*
   Belohnung, Anerkennung
to roam around (*or:* about)
   durchstreifen, umherwandern (in)
impression Eindruck
machine tools Werkzeugmaschinen
trade fairs (Handels-)
   Messen
to boast sich rühmen; *auch:*
   prahlen
to attract anziehen
to coincide zusammentreffen,
   zusammenfallen, sich
   decken (mit)
revenues Einnahmen, Einkünfte; *sonst auch:* Finanzverwaltung
to generate hervorbringen;
   sonst auch: erzeugen
host city gastgebende Stadt;
   host *auch:* Gastgeber

dominance Vorherrschaft, Dominanz
to claim meinen, behaupten; *sonst auch:* Anspruch erheben
to bill itself sich selbst bezeichnen
rented space vermietete Immobilien
to out-compete ausstechen
decent anständig, schicklich

The reward comes not only from tickets sold or space rented but from the boost the fairs give to the local economy. That helps Germany to out-compete France and Britain, where property owners expect a decent return.
Excerpt from The Economist, London

Relying on solar energy

to rely on sich stützen auf, verlassen, bauen auf
solar energy Sonnenenergie
turquoise türkisgrün
resort Erholungsort; *auch:* Zuflucht, Treffpunkt
to construct bauen
recycled wieder verwendet
crushed zerstoßen, zerdrückt
cardboard Pappe
rubber tire Gummireifen
scrap lumber Holzabfall
heat-reflective wärmereflektierend
to mount anbringen, befestigen, montieren
roof Dach
oven Herd; *auch:* Ofen
to operate on arbeiten mittels, werden betrieben mit
to feature als Besonderheit aufweisen
energy-efficient energiesparend
appliance (Haushalts-)Gerät
light bulb Glühlampe
occupancy sensor Steuerungsgerät (*auch:* Sensor) für die Raumbesetzung
to monitor überwachen

Sitting above the white beaches and turquoise waters of St. John in the Atlantic Ocean, the beautiful guesthouses seem like those of any typical tropical resort. But look again.

The buildings are constructed primarily of recycled materials: plastic bottles, crushed glass, newsprint, cardboard, rubber tires, steel and scrap lumber. The windows have heat-reflective glass. Photovoltaic collectors are mounted on the roofs.

The ovens are outside on the decks because they are solar powered. Welcome to Harmony, the world's first luxury resort to operate exclusively on sun and wind power. Set in the Virgin Islands National Park on the north shore of the smallest of the U.S. Virgins, each Harmony unit features energy-efficient appliances and light bulbs, occupancy sensors that turn off appliances after guests leave the room and a computer to monitor daily energy use. Eight guesthouses are now open.
TIME Newsmagazine, New York

Novel four-seat aircraft

Cirrus SR20 is the first four-seat aircraft with a parachute – for the whole plane. Mounted behind the cockpit and above the baggage area, the chute deploys only in worst-case scenarios, dropping the craft at 30 feet per second onto its landing gear.
Notes Chris Maddy of Cirrus Design, which plans to roll out the $ 144,500 planes next year: "It will wreck the airplane, you will be late for your appointment, but you will be safe."
U.S. News & World Report

novel neu(artig)
four-seat aircraft Viersitzer-Flugzeug
parachute Fallschirm
to mount anbringen, montieren, befestigen
baggage area Gepäckbereich
to deploy sich entfalten, einsetzen
worst-case für den schlimmsten Fall
scenario Szenario, Plan; *auch:* (Film-)Drehbuch
to drop fallen, niedergehen
landing gear Landegestell, Fahrwerk
to note meinen, angeben
to wreck zerstören, zum Wrack machen
appointment Verabredung, Termin

Synthetic diamonds for science and engineering

(1) Weighing in at a hefty 1600 carats, or at 320 grams, the world's largest synthetic diamond sounds as if it could outshine the crown jewels. But this diamond is disc-shaped, almost 30 centimetres in diameter and just 1.5 millimetres deep.
The diamond is made up of hundreds of smaller crystals rather than a single huge gem. "De Beers would look at this and say, "we have no worries," says James Adair, professor of materials science at the University of Florida, Gainesville. "But once you get past the romantic notions, diamond is one heck of an engineering material."

(1)
diamond Diamant
to weigh wiegen, wägen
hefty wuchtig, gewaltig, 'saftig'
to sound sich anhören, klingen, tönen
to outshine in den Schatten stellen, überstrahlen
disc-shaped scheibenförmig
diameter Durchmesser
gem Edelstein
materials science Materialwissenschaft

notion Vorstellung, Begriff,
  Gedanke
heck Teufelszeug; *sonst auch:*
  Hölle
(2)
abrasive Schleif…,
  Schmirgel…
coating Schicht, Überzug
machine tool Werkzeugmaschine
surface Oberfläche
to dissipate ableiten, abgeben;
  sonst auch: zerstreuen
silicon Silizium
layer Schicht, Lage
to enable ermöglichen, in den
  Stand setzen
to squeeze unterbringen; *auch:*
  quetschen, drücken
component Bauteil, Einzelteil,
  Komponente
to cause verursachen, bewirken
to improve verbessern
performance Leistung, Ver-
  mögen
vapour Dampf…, Ver-
  dampfungs…
deposition Ablagerung
(3)
to rely on beruhen auf
to deposit ablagern, setzen
carbon Kohlenstoff
substrate Grundlage, Unterlage
seed crystal Impfkristall,
  Kristallkeim
to provide vorsehen, liefern

(2) Because diamond is so hard, it makes an excellent abrasive or protective coating for everything from machine tools to kitchen surfaces.

And because it dissipates heat more rapidly than silicon, researchers would also like to build microchips on layers of diamond. This would enable them to squeeze more electronic components into a small area without causing overheating.

Adair and his colleague Rajiv Singh grew their diamond using a technique that radically improves the performance of chemical vapour deposition (CVD), the process normally used to grow industrial diamond coatings.

(3) There are several types of CVD, but they all rely on high temperature and low pressures to deposit carbon vapour as a layer of crystals on a surface or substrate.

The most difficult part of the process is getting crystals started. Tiny seed crystals must first be generated to provide the nuclei around which the larger crystals grow. Bubbles in a glass of champagne start in a similar way, growing from nuclei provided by tiny imperfections in the surface of the glass.

Excerpt from New Scientist, London

The all-purpose machine
we've come to depend on

Predicting the imminent demise of the personal computer has become an annual ritual in recent years, and each year the PC has defied the prophets of the doom.

This year looks set for a repeat performance.

Predictions for the first-quarter global sales were bad: the PC era was finally ending.

In fact, sales grew at 19 percent annual rate. Worldwide, well over 100 million PCs will be sold this year. That means the world now buys almost as much PCs as color TVs. Not surprising. Prices have fallen sharply. Consumers are rushing to get on the Web, and the PC makes that easy.

Excerpt from a feature article by Bill Gates, Newsweek, New York

all-purpose machine Allzweckmaschine
we've come to depend on von der wir nun alle abhängig sind
to predict voraussagen
imminent drohend, bevorstehend
demise Ableben; *sonst auch:* Besitzübertragung
to defy sich widersetzen, trotzen, die Stirn bieten
prophets of doom Untergangspropheten; **doom** *auch:* Verhängnis, Schicksal
it looks set for es sieht aus wie
repeat performance Wiederholungs-Vorführung
prediction Vorhersage
global sales Verkauf weltweit
era Ära, Zeitabschnitt
to rush sich beeilen, stürzen

Career guidance

(1) I have been looking over "Best jobs for the future." All you do is encourage more and more young people to get into white-collar jobs. Have you tried to get a plumber or an electrician lately?

Wake up! Unemployment lines are full of people who would hurt themselves if they tried to pick up a screwdriver. No wonder the Germans and Japanese are knocking the hell out of us. There is nothing wrong with getting your hand dirty. How do you think this country was built?

Kenneth E. Van Horn, Winslow, Ill.

(1)
career guidance Richtlinien für eine Karriere
to encourage ermutigen, anregen
white-collar job Büroberuf
plumber Klempner, Installateur
electrician Elektriker
unemployment lines Schlangen von Arbeitslosen
to hurt oneself sich wehtun; *oder:* verletzen

screwdriver Schraubenzieher
to knock the hell out of us
   uns die Hölle heiß machen
built (to build) gebaut
(2)
to speak volumes Bände
   sprechen
plight Notlage, Zwangslage
construction *hier:* Bauindustrie
manufacturing Herstellungsbetrieb, Verarbeitungsunternehmen
service jobs Arbeiten im
   Dienstleistungsbetrieb
to emphasize hervorheben;
   sonst auch: betonen,
   Schwergewicht legen auf
rewarding lohnend, profitabel;
   sonst auch: dankbar
beneficial förderlich, nutzbringend
to redistribute umverteilen,
   neuverteilen
available verfügbar, vorhanden
wealth-building Reichtum
   schaffend
decline Niedergang, Rückfall

(2) Your career guide speaks volumes about the economic plight of our nation. The only jobs that create wealth are in agriculture, mining, construction and manufacturing.

The service jobs you emphasize, no matter how personally rewarding or socially beneficial, can only redistribute the available wealth. Until wealth-building jobs are again honored and emphasized, our once great nation will continue its decline.

Dick Wingerson, Crested Butte, Colo.; from letters to the editor of Newsweek, New York

Message for computer users

message Meldung,
   Nachricht
user Benutzer, Anwender
to leave on eingeschaltet
   (ver)lassen
chip elektronischer Bauteil,
   Plättchen, Chip
to announce ankündigen, verkünden
to design konstruieren, entwerfen

Most office workers leave their computers on all day, but use them only 20 per cent of the time. The Intel Corporation, which makes the computer chips used in more than 75 per cent of all computers, has announced that all new models of their microchips are designed to put desktop computers into a "sleep" mode when they are not in use.

The typical desktop computer uses between 150 and 200 watts, but would use only thousandths of a watt in the standy mode.

The US Environmental Protection Agency esti-
mates that if the new "green chips" are provided
nationwide, they could cut annual electricity bills
by £1 billion by the year 2000, and significantly
reduce carbon dioxide pollution from electricity
generation.
Excerpt from U.S. News & World Report

desktop computer Tischcomputer
sleep mode "Schlafstellung"
standby mode Bereitschaftsstellung
**Environmental Protection
  Agency** Umweltschutz-
  behörde
to estimate schätzen
electricity bill Stromrechnung
significant bedeutend, bedeutsam
to reduce reduzieren, verringern
carbon dioxide Kohlenstoffdioxid
pollution (Umwelt-)Ver-
  schmutzung
electricity generation Elektrizitätserzeugung

Novel household-control system

(1) Many new dwelling places nowadays are touted as "smart homes." These houses and flats are
wired up with gadgetry turning the light and heating on or off, for example, or watering the lawn.
But they are not really all that smart, because
what they do is to follow a pre-ordained set of
instructions that tells the computer in charge
when to switch things on and off.
The instructions themselves still have to be pro-
grammed to suit individual tastes and desires, and
they have to be updated by hand if circumstances
change.
(2) Michael Mozer, a computer scientist at the
University of Colorado, thinks this is one of the
main reasons that home automation has not
caught on, despite decades of interest on the part
of both industry and consumers.

(1)
novel neu(artig)
household-control system
  Steuerungs- und Über-
  wachungsanlage für den
  Haushalt
dwelling place Wohnung,
  Wohnsitz
to tout anpreisen, aufdringliche Werbung
  betreiben
flat (Etagen-)Wohnung
to wire up verdrahten,
  anschließen
gadgetry Apparate, technische
  Spielereien
to turn on and off ein- und
  ausschalten
lawn Rasen

pre-ordained vorher eingestellt; **ordained** *sonst:* angeordnet, verfügt

computer in charge der zugeschaltete (*oder:* zuständige) Computer; **in charge** *sonst:* Leitung oder Führung innehaben

to suit tastes and desires dem Geschmack und den Wünschen gerecht werden

to update auf den neuesten Stand bringen

circumstances Bedingungen, Umstände

(2)

main reason Hauptgrund

not caught on (to catch on) sich nicht durchgesetzt, nicht an Boden gewonnen

decade Jahrzehnt

to reckon damit rechnen, halten für

to design konstruieren, entwerfen

genuine(ly) echt, wirklich

plumbing system Installationssystem (für Wasser, Gas usw.)

(3)

neural networks neurale Netze; **neural** *sonst:* Nerven…

habits Gewohnheiten

to anticipate sich darauf einstellen; *sonst:* erwarten

lit (to light) erleuchtet, beleuchtet

to consume verbrauchen

to suggest vermuten lassen; *sonst:* vorschlagen

to behave sich verhalten

brain Gehirn

What might change that, he reckons, is to get a house to program itself.

In fact, Dr Mozer himself lives in just such a house. Over the last few years, he and his students have designed and installed a genuinely smart heating, lighting, ventilation and plumbing system.

(3) The instructions about when to turn things on and off are not pre-programmed. Instead, Dr. Mozer's system uses neural networks. These learn his habits and so anticipate his needs in ways that keep the house heated and lit while consuming the minimum amount of energy.

Neural networks are computer programs that, as their name suggests, behave rather like nerve cells in an animal's brain.

(4) When a natural nerve network learns something, the connections between the individual cells change in ways that cause the animal to react more suitably in the future. Artificial neural networks operate in a similar fashion, altering the strength of connections between different parts of a program in response to experience, so as to achieve the desired result. They are particularly good at recognising patterns and working out relationships.

Dr. Mozer's household control system consists of a number of different neural networks, each in charge of one aspect of his domestic economy. It works so well that Dr Mozer says, that he misses it terribly when it is turned off.

Excerpt from The Economist, London

How to tackle the corporate problems

Ministry of Progress Strategic Branch

Brilliant people of the MinProg Strategic Branch are never at a loss. They create situations no enemy would ever think of.

(4)
to cause verursachen, bewirken
suitable (-bly) angemessen; *sonst auch:* passend, geeignet
artificial künstlich
to operate arbeiten, werden betrieben
fashion Weise
to alter verändern
in response to in Reaktion auf
experience Erfahrung
to achieve erreichen, gelangen zu
result Ergebnis, Resultat
to recognise (wieder)erkennen
pattern Muster
relationship Beziehung
to consist of bestehen aus

Radio telescopes for "interstellar TV"

Astronomy is a science that requires enormous and expensive playthings, so its practitioners can be forgiven for using a little hype to encourage its paymasters (meaning taxpayers) to reach into their pockets when a new toy again is needed.
But their latest gambit is still pretty breathtaking: "Give us half a billion dollars and you might be able to watch interstellar TV."
The toy that would allow this – assuming, that is, that any neighbouring solar systems have actually developed TV-watching civilisations – is a putative radio telescope known as the Square Kilometre Array (SKA).
This would also allow the world's radio astronomers to study such things as radio waves from the first stars to form after the Big Bang.

interstellar zwischen den Sternen befindlich
to require benötigen, erfordern
plaything Spielzeug
practitioner Praktizierende(r)
hype Trick, Finesse
to encourage ermutigen
taxpayer Steuerzahler
gambit raffinierter Trick; *sonst auch:* Einleitung
breathtaking atemberaubend
able imstande; *auch:* fähig
to assume annehmen, vermuten
actual(ly) tatsächlich
to develop entwickeln

putative vermeintlich, putativ
array *(im Namen)* Anordnung, Reihe
to form sich bilden, formieren
task Aufgabe
to turn into verwandeln in
radio dish "Antennenschüssel"
area Fläche, Gebiet
feasible durchführbar
to add together zusammen-schalten, -fügen

At the moment it is only a "paper" instrument. But two meetings of high-powered radio astronomers held in the Netherlands over the past few weeks, one in Amsterdam and the other in Dwingeloo, have begun the task of turning it into metal.

Of course, a single radio dish with an area as big as one quare kilometre is not feasible. A multi-dish design, a "collecting area," would be required. A computer will add together the signals from sub-telescopes.

Excerpt from The Economist, London

Refuelling hydrogen or fuel cells

refuelling (Wieder-)Auftanken
hydrogen Wasserstoff
fuel cell Brennstoffzelle
to turn into verwandeln in
to require benötigen, erfordern
to convert umwandeln, ver-wandeln in
it must exact a toll es muß einen Tribut zollen; **to exact** *auch:* (Zahlung) einfordern, eintreiben; **toll** *auch:* (Brü-cken-)Zoll, (Hafen-)Gebühr
to occur vorkommen, auftreten
petrol *GB:* Benzin (*US:* **gaso-line**)
step-by-step stufenweise
transition Übergang; *sonst auch:* Durchgang
economy Wirtschaft(lichkeit)
to adopt übernehmen, anneh-men
letter to the editor Leserbrief
to go astray vom Weg abkom-men, das Ziel verfehlen

Turning water into hydrogen takes a lot more energy than turning hydrogen back into water, of course; otherwise it would be a perpetuum mobile. Thermodynamics requires that converting any energy form into another, such as coal into elec-tricity, must exact a toll.

And, of course, hydrogen fuel does not normally occur in nature any more than does petrol. A step-by-step-transition to a practical hydrogen eco-nomy is already being adopted by some large energy and car companies.

Here Mr Bevec's logic (letter to the editor) goes astray in comparing hydrogen's energy content of that of fossil fuels as if it would simply be burnt. An unworthy goal, as there are far more effective ways to convert hydrogen into useful work.

The best fuel cell can turn hydrogen into car motion about four times as efficiently as a normal car engine, or into electricity twice as efficiently as a classical power station and grid; three or more times when the fuel cell's heat also provides valuable building services.

That is why well-designed hydrogen systems yield major savings in fuel, climate risk and money, as well as conventional pollution. Hydrogen fuel cells have no combustion and emit only drinking water.

By Amory Lovins, Rocky Mountain Institute, Snowmass, Colorado; The Economist, London

to compare vergleichen
energy content Energiegehalt
unworthy nicht vertretbar, unwürdig
goal Ziel
motion Bewegung
efficient(ly) wirksam, effizient
car engine Automotor
power station Kraftwerk
grid Verbundnetz
to provide vorsehen, liefern
valuable wertvoll
to design konstruieren, auslegen
to yield ergeben, hervorbringen
major savings wesentliche Einsparungen
pollution Umweltverschmutzung
combustion Verbrennung
to emit abgeben, emittieren

And please let me have a copy of this message.

Foreign engineers in Russia and the Russian customs

One of the earliest and most educative experiences western engineers and managers have in Moscow comes when their possessions pass through Russian customs. Unlike almost any other country, Russia levies import duties, sometimes to the tune of several thousand dollars, on ordinary household removals.

But the latest move by the Russian customs service is making even hardened expatriates blench. In the past, foreign business offices were allowed to import cars, computers and so forth dutyfree, on the understanding that they would eventually re-export them. As from April 1st, this has been cancelled, in a way which leaves foreign compa-

customs 1. Gewohnheiten, 2. Zoll(ämter)
educative erzieherisch; *sonst:* sich bildend
experiences 1. Erfahrungen, 2. Erlebnisse
possessions Besitz(tümer)
to pass through customs durch den Zoll gehen
to levy (Abgaben oder Gebühren) erheben
duties *hier:* Abgaben
to the tune of in der Höhe von, man sage und schreibe

household removal Umzug mit dem (ganzen) Haushalt

move *hier:* Schritt

expatriate im Ausland lebender Staatsbürger

to blench zurückschrecken

eventual(ly) schließlich, letzten Endes

to cancel aufgeben, streichen

allowance for depreciation Billigung zur Abschreibung

representative office Büro eines (Firmen-)Vertreters

to pay duty Zoll zahlen

nies with potential costs of tens of millions of dollars.

Nor does the customs regime make any allowance for depreciation. In other words, a foreign representative office which has already imported a 1995 Land Rover will now have to pay duty on it, and the original price ($ 29,000), rather than its current value ($ 12,000).

Excerpt from The Economist, London

Engineers revive the airship era

to revive wieder aufleben lassen; *sonst auch:* wiederbeleben

era Ära, Zeitabschnitt

took off (to take off) abhob

decade Jahrzehnt

succession Fortführung, Folgezeit

ambitious ehrgeizig

craft Luftschiff, Flugzeug oder Fahrzeug allgemein

to culminate in Spitze erreichen mit (*oder:* in)

to launch starten; *sonst auch:* (Schiff) vom Stapel lassen

crossing Überquerung

heyday Höhepunkt, Gipfel, Blütezeit

hydrogen Wasserstoff

to burst into flames in Flammen aufgehen

proponent Befürworter, Anhänger

When Count von Zeppelin took off in his first airship on July 22nd 1900, it seemed that the flying machine of the future had arrived. The next few decades saw a succession of ever larger and more ambitious craft, culminating in the 245-metre (800 foot) Hindenburg, which was launched in 1936.

The Hindenburg could carry as many as 120 people. Indeed, it made several transatlantic crossings. But the heyday of these graceful flying machines came soon to an end when the Hindenburg – filled, like most airships that time, with explosive hydrogen – burst into flames in 1937.

Airship enthusiasts have been trying to pick up the pieces ever since. Modern proponents of the technology dream of a new generation of the machines, buoyed by inert helium rather than by hydrogen, and taking advantage of space-age materials and modern avionics.

There are now signs that the long-mooted airship revival is starting. A handful of firms around the world have begun work on large airships, comparable in size to the great Zeppelins of the 1930s. Aiming at new markets in freight and luxury travel, they hope to fly within two years. The furthest-advanced of the new airship companies, a German-American firm called Cargo Lifter, is planning a 260-metre-long airship that is intended to lift goods, not passengers. Lifting capacity shall be 160 tonnes.

Excerpt from The Economist, London

to buoy by betreiben mittels
to take advantage die Vorteile nutzen
avionics Elektronik der Luftfahrt
long-mooted schon lange diskutiert
revival Wiederaufleben
comparable vergleichbar
to aim at (ab)zielen auf
freight Fracht
furthest-advanced am weitesten fortgeschritten
to intend beabsichtigen
lifting capacity Tragvermögen

Amphibious vehicles in unsafe waters

Ancient amphibious vehicles known as "ducks" are a common sight in American waterside tourist spots. Moving at up to 50 mph on land but only 6 mph on water, they are supposed to be safe. They sink slowly. But the duck that sank last month on Lake Hamilton, outside Hot Springs in Arkansas, disappeared in less than a minute.

In a country bound to rules about everything, water safety is a surprising exception. An Arkansas law dictates that children under 13 must wear a life jacket when riding in a moving boat, unless it is a houseboat.

But the ducks, which are military equipment from the second world war, are regulated by the Coastguard, which does not insist on life jackets for passengers. The relevant law, of 1930, simply states that a boat must carry "readily accessible" jackets for everyone on board.

amphibious vehicle Amphibien-Fahrzeug
ancient alt, altertümlich
common sight gewohnter Anblick
spot Stelle, Platz
mph (miles per hour) Meilen pro Stunde
to suppose annehmen, vermuten
to disappear verschwinden
bound to rules an Vorschriften gebunden
law Gesetz
to wear a life jacket eine Schwimmweste tragen
equipment Ausrüstung, Gerät(e)
does not insist on besteht nicht darauf
relevant zutreffend, gültig
to state angeben, bestimmen

readily accessible leicht zugänglich
operators *hier:* Betreiber
to require erfordern, benötigen
federal law Bundesgesetz
customer Kunde
accident Unfall
to alter opinion Meinung
ändern

Operators are not keen to see jackets required
under federal law, because customers dislike
wearing them. But last month's accident may
alter opinion.
Excerpt from The Economist, London

Cross-Channel bootlegging

Cross-Channel bootlegging
Schmuggel bei Kanalüber-
querung
scruffy *(Sl.)* schmuddelig
a.m. (Lat.) ante meridiem:
before noon
p.m. (Lat.) post meridiem:
after noon
van Lieferwagen
estate car Familienauto
number plate Nummernschild
to load beladen
hand-rolling Handroll…
wads of notes Banknoten-
Bündel
villainous-looking schurkisch
aussehend
to strip entfernen, runterreißen
pouch großer Beutel, Sack
bin bag Behältertaschen
space Platz, Raum
odd curse *etwa:* hin und wieder zu hörendes Fluchen
stranger Fremder
to accept annehmen, akzeptieren
retail price Preis im Einzelhandel
to roar off davondonnern
(*oder:* -röhren)
to account for ausmachen

Adinkerke, a small, scruffy Belgian village near
the French border, 54 km (33 miles) from Calais,
never sleeps. Even at 3 a.m., there are lines of
white vans and estate cars with British number plates
being loaded with huge quantities of hand-rolling
tobacco bought with wads of British notes.
Inside the warehouses, teams of villainous-looking characters are stripping the packaging and
putting tobacco pouches into large black bin bags
to save space. Apart from the odd curse, there is
not a lot of chat. Questions from strangers are
unwelcome. A box of hand-rolling tobacco holds
100 50-gramme (1.8-ounce) pouches.
The cost per box in Adinkerke, only sterling
accepted, is £199 ($318) compared with a retail
price in Britain of £785. The laden vehicles roar
off towards Calais to catch the next ferry to
Dover. The cost for an estate car leaving Dover
before 7 a.m. and returning on the same day is a
mere £10.
There are eight tobacco warehouses in the village,
five of which are open 24 hours a day. Today,
already two-thirds of the British market in hand-
rolling tobacco is accounted for by illegal im-
ports.
Excerpt from The Economist, London

London Heathrow Airport

Travelers at Heathrow Airport need no longer rush from one counter to another finalizing flight details and booking hotel room and rental cars.

Instead, they can stroll up to a WAMworld Web kiosk and do it all without moving another inch. The kiosks' touch screens allow travelers to request a seat, access the websites of companies that advertise in the airport, send flowers or even e-mail, hire a car – and if they're cautious, buy insurance.

TIME Newsmagazine, New York

to rush stürzen, stürmen, dahinjagen
counter Schalter
to stroll up bummeln, schlendern, (spazieren)gehen
without moving another inch ohne sich einen Zoll weiterzubewegen
touch screen Kontaktbildschirm
to request erfragen, veranlassen, bitten (um)
access Zugang, Zutritt
to advertise werben, inserieren
insurance Versicherung

A special 15th April for U.S. citizens

This 15th April is a day that fills many Americans with dread. It's the deadline for sending in their tax returns.

Everyone in the U.S. has to return the Internal Revenue Services' form 1040. And in recent years, the process has been made easier.

You can now file your tax return by post or by e-mail. For those who are confused by the change, the IRS has some helpful advice.

The back of the envelope it sends out for people to return their forms in reads: "If you are filing electronically, do not use this envelope."

By the way, this date is to remember for a human catastrophe: On 15th April 1912 the luxury steamer Titanic sank hundred miles off Newfoundland.

Feedback in New Scientist, London

citizen Staatsbürger
to fill with dread mit großer Angst erfüllen; **dread** *auch:* Grauen
deadline letzter Termin, Fristablauf
tax return Steuererklärung
Internal Revenue Services Steuerbehörde
to file the tax die Steuererklärung einreichen
confused verwirrt, irritiert
advice Rat(schlag)
envelope Kuvert

Saxony – turned into a high-tech state

to turn into sich wandeln zu;
auch: sich verwandeln in
publishing Verlagswesen
to predict vorhersagen
area Gebiet, Umgebung
valley of the clueless Tal der
Ahnungslosen
to tune into hereinbekommen,
sehen können
to create schaffen, kreieren
silicon *(im Namen)* Silizium
to spend ausgeben, investieren
on a greenfield plant in einer
Anlage im Grünen
eventual(ly) schließlich, letzten Endes
to employ beschäftigen
ventures Unternehmungen
fast-growing schnellwachsend
chose (to choose) wählte
research and development
hub Zentrum für Forschung
und Entwicklung;
hub *sonst auch:* Angelpunkt, (Rad-)Nabe

Hamburg has its publishing, Frankfurt its centre of finance; might Saxony become known for high technology? Saxony? The idea is rather like predicting a new Silicon Valley in downtown Detroit.

Indeed, the low-lying area around its capital, Dresden, was known in East German times as the "valley of the clueless," because locals could not tune into western television. Yet today, it is also the east's best hope of creating a valley of the silicon kind.

The area has seen a wave of investment by western technology firms. AMD, an American microchip maker, is spending $1.9 billion on a greenfield plant that will eventually employ 1,800 people. Siemens and Motorola, between them, have hired more than 2,500 people for their own chip ventures.

This year Mattson Technology, a fast-growing Californian firm, even chose Dresden as its research and development hub for Europe.
Excerpt from The Economist, London

Towards California's zero-emissions law

toward(s) hin zum
zero-emissions law Gesetz,
betreffend schadstofflose
Abgase
to desire wünschen
manufacturer Farbikant
to grasp fassen; *sonst auch:*
packen, ergreifen

"I sell here, Sir, what all the world desires to have. Power." Matthew Boulton, the manufacturer who made James Watt's steam engine into an industrial tool, grasped the realities of the new industrial revolution from the beginning.

For 100 years, the source of power was coal. For almost another 100 it has been oil. But, as the revolution that Boulton helped to start, enters its third century; it may be about to embrace a third fuel: hydrogen.

The idea of a "hydrogen economy," in which that light, combustible gas would be the main source of energy, has been around for several decades. It was dreamed up by people who wondered what would happen when the oil ran out.

In the way of predictions about the future, those people tended to extrapolate from the present. Hydrogen would be used in the same way that petrol and its cousins are: burned in engines. That however, is not going to happen. Instead, not only will fuel change, so will the engines that it powers. Hydrogen, when burned, produces water. And fuel cells do not even burn it; the reaction in a fuel cell has no flame, so noxious by-products such as nitrogen oxides are impossible.

Fuel-cell-powered vehicles would thus, in the jargon, be "zero-emissions" vehicles as demanded by California's zero-emissions law.

Excerpt from The Economist, London

source of power Energiequelle
to enter beginnen, eintreten in
to embrace erfassen, aufnehmen; *sonst auch:* umschließen, umarmen
hydrogen Wasserstoff
combustible brennbar
decade Jahrzehnt
when the oil ran out wenn das Öl zur Neige gehen würde
prediction Vorhersage
to tend dazu neigen
petrol Benzin; *US:* gasoline
engine (Verbrennungs-)Motor
fuel Brennstoff, Treibstoff
fuel cell Brennstoffzelle
noxious giftig, Schadstoff...
by-product Nebenprodukt
nitrogen oxides Stickstoffoxide
to demand fordern, verlangen

Creating Websites

Planning to put up your own website? Need a good how-to guide? Begin with the new book: Creating Killer Websites, by David Siegel, Hayden Books, $ 55, ISBN 1568304331.

It should be mandatory reading for everyone who publishes on the Web. Well written and designed, it is packed with practical advice, clear illustrations and a warning list for deadly sins. Siegel deals with principles so the book should not date even when technologies change. It is opinionated, provocative, witty and right. Can you imagine a book on tech-

to create herstellen, schaffen, kreieren
to put up aufbauen, einrichten
how-to guide Richtlinien für, Berater
mandatory vorgeschrieben, ein Muß
to publish veröffentlichen
to design aufbauen, konstruieren, entwerfen
advice Ratschlag, Hinweis
deadly sins Todsünden

to deal with behandeln, zu tun haben mit
should not date *etwa:* es sollte auch weiterhin lesenswert sein; sollte zeitlich nicht begrenzt sein
opinionated dogmatisch, schulmeisterlich, überheblich
to acquire (käuflich) erwerben

nology that has made you laughing out loud? Anyone who thinks the book is dead should acquire this one.
Excerpt from The Economist, London

Engineering profession in America

engineering profession der Beruf des Ingenieurs
society Gesellschaft
increasing(ly) immer mehr, wachsend
dependent on abhängig von
flourishing gedeihend, blühend
layoff (vorübergehende) Entlassung, Freisetzung
corporate recruiting Anwerbung durch Firmen
to decide sich entscheiden
graduate degree Grad von einer Universität oder Fachhochschule (university or college)
professional edge Vorteil (*oder:* Vorsprung) im Berufsleben; **edge** *sonst:* Schneide, Kante
to earn erwerben, verdienen
M.S. *Master of Science:* Magister der Naturwissenschaften
Ph.D. *Philosophy Doctor:* Dr. der Philosophie
shortage Mangel, Bedarf, Knappheit
surplus Überfluss, Überschuss

In a society increasingly dependent on technology, the engineering profession is flourishing. The number of engineers in the United States is now 2 million, an all-time record.

Companies at which layoffs had become a way of life are hiring once again. Corporate recruiting is up at many schools. In short, it is a seller market.

For those deciding whether a graduate degree will give them a professional edge, however,

the question is not what the job market is today but what it will be after they have earned an M.S. or Ph.D. After all, history shows that the job market for engineers in particular specialties moves from shortage to surplus as rapidly as the wave cycles in an oscilloscope.

The most popular specialty today is electrical engineering. Experts say demand will stay high for EE's.

The computer and the telecommunications industries will also need systems engineers who can look at the big picture and getting the most out of complex networks. The rise of the Internet should open up a number of new opportunities as well, says Frank Huband, CEO of the American Society of Engineering Education.

Excerpt from U.S. News & World Report

Since he tasted that aluminium alloy he won't touch greens any more.

Artist's impression of creepy crawlies employed at the research laboratory, Ministry of Progress, Pulham Down.

wave cycle Wellenzyklus
demand Bedarf; *sonst auch:* Forderung
rise Ansteigen, Vergrößerung
opportunities Möglichkeiten, Gelegenheiten
CEO *chief executive officer; etwa:* Generaldirektor
engineering education technische Ausbildung

Boeing's engineering feat

Thirty years ago, the first 747 plane went into commercial service and changed the way of air travel. This craft accelerated an air-travel revolution ushered in by the first successful jetliner, the Boeing 707, in 1958. With as many as 550 seats to fill on some 747 flights, airlines could cut the price of a ticket.

People saw the chance to become international travelers for the first time. Businessmen had greater access to markets in Europe and the Far East. Thanks to the plane's air-freight capacity, fresh flowers and produce became staples in the cities where they'd previously been available only in season.

William E. Boeing, founder of the company that designed the 747, built his first plane in 1916. He had to resort to manufacturing bedroom furniture to survive some lean years.

But he persevered, and the Boeing Airplane Co. in Seattle went on to build thousands of military craft. The Boeing 707 was a marvel of its day.

It could carry 181 passengers nonstop from New York to Paris. But by 1965, airlines were pressing for a 400-passenger plane that could fly farther, faster.

engineering feat technische Großtat; **feat** *auch:* Meisterstück, Kraftakt
craft *hier:* Flugzeug; *sonst:* Fahrzeug allgemein
to accelerate beschleunigen
to usher in einleiten
access Zugang, Zutritt
air-freight capacity Luftfracht, Aufnahmevermögen
produce *hier:* Naturprodukte, Bodenprodukte
staple Haupterzeugnis, Stapelware
previous(ly) vorher, früher
available zu haben, verfügbar
founder Gründer
to design konstruieren
to resort to zurückgreifen auf; *auch:* sich neu orientieren
bedroom furniture Schlafzimmermöbel
to survive überleben, überstehen
lean mager
to persevere durchhalten, festhalten an
to build bauen

marvel Wunder(ding)
cruise at fliegen in … Höhe
mph *(miles per hour)* Meilen pro Stunde
refueling Nachtanken

For Boeing it was testing time. So they were building the famous 747 for 400 passengers, cruise at 35,000 feet, go about 625 mph and fly 5000 miles without refueling.

Excerpt from a Boeing feature article, Seattle

Charles Babbage – a computer pioneer

exasperated verärgert, wütend gemacht, aufgebracht
error Fehler, Irrtum
table *hier:* Tabelle
widely used weit verbreitet, weit genutzt
calculation aids Rechnungshilfen
to build bauen
device Gerät
flawless fehlerfrei, fehlerlos
attempt Versuch
to fail fehlschlagen, danebengehen
significance Bedeutung, Bedeutsamkeit
rediscovered wiederentdeckt
to emerge kommen aus; *sonst auch:* auftauchen, erscheinen
calculating machine Rechenmaschine, Rechner
design *hier:* Konstruktionsplan
to vindcate Anspruch geltend machen
to underscore unterstreichen, betonen
extent *hier:* Größe, Außergewöhnliches
ahead of his time seiner Zeit voraus
effort Anstrengung, Bemühen
to prove beweisen

Success, it is often said, has many fathers – and one of the many fathers of computing was Charles Babbage, a 19th century mathematician.

Exasperated by errors in the mathematical tables that were widely used as calculation aids at the time, Babbage dreamed of building a device that could produce flawless tables automatically. But his attempts to make such a machine in the 1820s failed, and the significance of his work was only rediscovered this century.

Next year, at last, the first set of printed tables should emerge from a calculating machine built to Baggage's design. Babbage will have been vindicated. But the realisation of his dream will also underscore the extent to which was a man born ahead of his time.

The effort to prove that Babbage's designs were logically and practically sound began in 1985, when a team of researchers at the Science Museum in London set out to build a difference machine in time for the 200th anniversary of Babbage's birth in 1992. The team, led by the museum's curator of computing, Doron Swade, constructed a monstrous device of bronze, iron and steel. It was 11 feet long, seven feet tall, weighed three tons, cost around £300,000 and took a year to piece together. And it worked perfectly.

Excerpt from The Economist, London

There has been an alarming increase in the number of things I know nothing about.

sound richtig; *sonst auch:* gesund
researcher Forscher
to set out sich dranmachen, beginnen
anniversary Jahrestag, jährlicher Gedenktag
to construct *hier:* bauen
to weigh wiegen
to piece together zusammensetzen

The English language and the Internet secure servers

Languages other than English account for only 2% of all pages linked to secure servers. Why is English so prominent? After all it has become clear that people prefer Internet services in their own language. But if you are trying to sell something and to use the Internet to reach a global market, then a Webpage in English will not only reach those whose first language is English, but the even larger number of people for whom English is their second language.
Excerpt from The Economist, London

secure server *etwa:* Anschluß an sichere Bedieneinheit
to account for ausmachen, betragen
to link verbinden
prominent hervorstechend, führend
to prefer bevorzugen
to reach erreichen

What did you say?

A high-volume world takes a toll on ever younger ears. Everyday life is growing noisier and as it does, more Americans are losing their hearing sooner.
Long accustomed to treating senior citizens, a growing number of hearing specialists now report that patients in their 40s and 50s, and sometimes even in their teens, are turning up in their

high-volume world zu lärmige Welt, Welt voller Lärm
to take a toll Tribut fordern, arg mitnehmen
to lose the hearing das Gehör verlieren
to accustom to sich gewöhnen an
to treat behandeln

senior citizens ältere Bürger
to report berichten
to turn up erscheinen, auftauchen
to complain sich beschweren
to sound sich anhören, tönen,
   klingen
to expect erwarten
observation Beobachtung
to bolster stärken, unterstützen; *sonst auch:*
   (aus)polstern
survey statistische Erhebung,
   Untersuchung

waitrooms. They complain that things don't sound as clear as they should.

"I see middle-aged patients," says Professor Dr. Thomas Balkany, University of Miami, "who have the kind of hearing we'd expect to see in their parents."

Statistics are starting to bolster the expert's observations. The National Health Survey shows that from 1971 to 1997, hearing problems shot up 26 % – by ages 45 to 64.

Excerpt from U.S. News & World Report

Answering the telephone

to answer the telephone
   Hörer abnehmen, Telefon
   beantworten
methodical(ly) methodisch,
   überlegt
last name Nachname
curious neugierig
caller Anrufer
inscrutable unergründlich
to proclaim ausrufen, verkünden

When Americans answer the telephone, they say "Hello." Not so in other countries. Germans methodically answer with their last names.

Russians say, "I'm listening." The French say, "Hello, who's on the line?", Italians greet callers with "Ready," the staid English answer with their phone number, and the inscrutable Chinese proclaim, "Hey, hey, who are you?"

From The Chicagoer

Transmission-line towers, telegraph poles and lighting

transmission-line tower
   Leitungsmast für Strom-
   übetragung
telegraph pole Telegrafenmast;
   pole *auch:* Stange, Pfahl
lighting Beleuchtung
to suggest hinweisen, hindeuten; *sonst auch:* vorschlagen

I have suggsted in the past that one day people will be as nostalgic about transmission-line towers as they are today about windmills and old steam trains.

Sir Peter Medawar expressed such a thought in a course of his presidential address of the British Association at Exeter, but he also said rather dubiously:

"For some people even the smell of telegraphic poles is nostalgic though the creosote has a pretty technological smell. Telegraph poles have been assimilated into the common consciousness and one day pylons will be, too.

When the pylons are dismantled and the cables finally all go underground, people will think again of those majestic curves and remind each other of how giants once marched across the counryside in dead silence and single file."

While on this subject I may mention one thing which has already become a coveted reminder of the fairly recent past: the gas lamp. There is a ready sale for these obsolete objects.

The Northern Echo says that towns which now form Teeside were lit by 12,000 gas lamps. When they were superseded by electric light several people bought them for their garden decorations powered by electricity.

Brian Hansson, Electrical Review, London

to express ausdrücken
in a course of während
presidential address *hier:* Ansprache nach der Wahl zum Präsidenten
dubious(ly) zweifelnd; *sonst auch:* fragwürdig, unbestimmt
smell Geruch
to assimilate *hier:* eindringen; *sonst:* angleichen, anpassen, assimilieren
common consciousness allgemeines Bewußtsein
pylon (freitragender) Mast
to dismantle abbauen, demontieren
giant Gigant
in single file in einer Reihe
coveted reminder begehrtes Erinnerungsstück
obsolete veraltet, altmodisch
to supersede ersetzen; *sonst auch:* abschaffen, beseitigen

Corporate discretion

A large engineering company was looking for a replacement for one of their top officials, who was going to retire. Among the candidates who were short-listed was one who seemed to fit the company's requirements in every way.

The chairman was delighted. "We'll interview him just for the sake of form," he said, "but I don't think we need look further."

"There's just one thing, though," said one of the members of the committee. "I don't know Mr. Westhouse personally. But I have heard that he is inclined to lift his elbow a deal too much. We should make a point of finding out whether this is true."

corporate das Unternehmen betreffend; *sonst auch:* Körperschafts…
discretion Umsicht, Besonnenheit
replacement Ersetzung, Ersatz
top official Chef an der Spitze
to retire in den Ruhestand treten
short-listed auf der Auswahlliste, obenan
to fit the requirements den Anforderungen gerecht werden

chairman Vorsitzender
delighted begeistert, 'entzückt'
for the sake of form nur so,
   als Formsache
member Mitglied
he is inclined er neigt dazu
to lift the elbow a deal too
   much gern einen zuviel
   heben
to make a point es darauf anlegen
to usher hineinführen
concerning betreffend
experience Erfahrung
to suggest *hier:* bedeuten;
   sonst: vorschlagen
unhesitating(ly) ohne zu
   zögern
immediate(ly) sofort
Commander-in-Chief Ober-
   befehlshaber
baffled verwirrt, verblüfft
pope Papst

The day came for the interview. Mr. Westhouse was ushered before the committee. The chairman asked a few questions concerning personal details and work experience.

Then he said, "Now, Mr. Westhouse, we would like to ask you a few questions of a different nature. The first is: what does the word 'Haig' suggest to you?" Unhesitatingly Mr. Westhouse replied, "I immediately recall the famous Commander-in-Chief Earl Haig."

"Thank you," said the chairman. "And the word 'White Horse.'?" "The beautiful Vale of White Horse in Oxfordshire where I have spent many happy days." "Splendid," said the chairman. "Just one last question. What are your reactions to the words VAT 69?"

Mr. Westhouse looked a bit baffled. "Ah, there you have me, I'm afraid. Could it be the Pope's telephone number?"

Electronics & Power, Stevenage, England

Tower of power

furnace Industrieofen,
   Hochofen
mill Fabrik, Mühle
foundry Gießerei
to fuel betreiben, antreiben;
   sonst auch: Öl bunkern, auftanken
built (to build) gebaut
striking auffallend, Eindruck
   machend
to survive überleben, standhalten
decline Niedergang, Rückgang
to doom *hier:* aufgeben, verloren gehen lassen

For its furnaces, mills and foundries, the German Ruhrgebiet was named "the land of thousand fires." Many flames were fueled by Europe's largest gas container, the Oberhausen gasometer. Built in 1929, it was the region's most striking industrial landmark and survived World War II bombing. The Ruhr's economic decline since the 1970s seemed to doom the 115-m-tall structure until an ambitious urban renewal project invested $10 million to transform it into a center for cultural and industrial exhibits.

Looming among the construction cranes on a site where land is being cleared for an impressive $1.3 billion shopping center with parks and marina, the gasometer is a veritable cathedral of industry.

Entering at ground level, visitors can look all way at ground level, visitors can look all the way to the top, where a shaft of light enters.

Up several steps is the formerly movable lid that could once hold down 347,000 cu m of gas.

Now fixed at 4 m high, it provides space to display items documenting two centuries of Ruhrgebiet history.

Mining equipment, drilling machines, Krupp-made cannons and computers are on display, as are photos, maps and testimony.

Time Newsmagazine, New York

structure Bau(werk)
ambitious ehrgeizig, anspruchsvoll
urban renewal project Stadt-erneuerungsvorhaben
to transform into verwandeln in
to loom along aufragen über; *sonst auch:* von Bedeutung sein (bei, über)
exhibit Ausstellung, Ausstellungsstück
site Standort; *auch:* Baustelle
veritable wirklich, echt
shaft Schacht; *sonst auch:* Welle
lid Abdeckung, Deckel
to provide vorsehen, liefern
mining equipment Bergbau-ausrüstung

Geothermal power in Britain

Experts believe Britain has the potential to produce 10 % of its electricity for 3,000 years by forcing water through hot rocks deep underground.

Many countries are exploring ways of tapping geothermal energy, either by using hot water from underground lakes to warm buildings directly, or by extracting heat from dry rocks as feedwater for local power stations. The British Department of Energy instigated a program to drill in promising areas.

Bore holes have now been drilled in four different parts of Britain under this project.

The Week, London

to produce erzeugen
to force drücken, zwingen
rocks Felsgestein
to explore erforschen, erkunden
to tap entnehmen, (ab)zapfen
to extract entziehen, entnehmen
feedwater Speisewasser
power station Kraftwerk
Department of Energy Ministerium für Energieerzeugung
to instigate anfachen; *sonst auch:* anstiften, aufhetzen
to drill bohren
promising (viel)versprechend
area Gebiet, Bereich

Letter openings

Thank you very much for your immediate reply to our questions.
Wir danken Ihnen sehr für die sofortige Beantwortung unserer Fragen.

We are very pleased to note from your letter of 2nd May ...
Wir freuen uns, aus Ihrem Brief vom 2. Mai zu erfahren, ...

Thank you very much for your letter of 20th May regarding ...
Vielen Dank für Ihren Brief vom 20. Mai betreffend ...

In reply to your letter of 3rd April, we have pleasure in offering you ...
Wir freuen uns, Ihnen gemäß Brief vom 3. April ... anbieten zu können.

We regret to learn from your report ...
Wir bedauern, Ihrem Bericht entnehmen zu müssen, ...

In response to your request of 19th May, I would advise you ...
Entsprechend Ihrer Anfrage vom 19. Mai möchte ich Ihnen mitteilen (*auch:* empfehlen, anraten), ...

I am delighted to tell you ...
Es freut mich, Ihnen mitteilen zu könnnen, ...

This is to let you know ...
Hiermit möchten wir Sie informieren, ...

I am sorry to have to tell you ...
Es tut mir leid, Ihnen mitteilen zu müssen, ...

I must write you a few words of thanks for ...
Ich muss Ihnen ein paar Worte des Dankes für ... schreiben.

Thanking you for your above mentioned enquiry, we take pleasure in quoting you for ...
Wir danken Ihnen für die oben erwähnte Anfrage und möchten Ihnen folgendes Angebot unterbreiten ...

In accordance with your request, we submit the following quotation.
Gemäß Ihrer Anfrage übersenden wir die folgende Offerte.

We have much pleasure in attaching ...
Es freut uns, Ihnen als Beilage ... übersenden zu können.

Please submit additional data providing the background information and parameters which went into this calculation.
Übersenden Sie bitte weitere grundsätzliche Angaben und Parameter, die in dieser Berechnung zugrunde gelegt worden sind.

This letter confirms our verbal acceptance given to you on 5th May at your offices.
Mit diesem Brief bestätigen wir unsere mündliche Zusage vom 5. Mai in Ihrem Hause.

Following a discussion with your Mr. Jones on ... at ...
Gemäß einer Diskussion mit Ihrem Herrn Jones am ... in ...

Would you be so kind as to allow me to bring this matter to your notice.
Gestatten Sie bitte, dass ich mich in dieser Angelegenheit an Sie wende.

Letter endings

We trust that we have been of some assistance in this matter.
Wir hoffen, dass wir Ihnen in dieser Angelegenheit etwas Unterstützung geben konnten.

If you require any further information, please do not hesitate to contact us.
Falls Sie weitere Angaben benötigen, so setzen Sie sich bitte unverzüglich mit uns in Verbindung.

We shall be glad to supply any further information which may be required.
Gern übersenden wir Ihnen weitere Angaben, soweit erforderlich.

Thanking you in anticipation for ...
Vielen Dank im voraus für ...

We should be glad if you would accept our proposals and hope to hear from you soon.
Wir würden uns freuen, wenn Sie unsere Vorschläge annehmen könnten, und hoffen, von Ihnen bald wieder etwas zu hören.

We look forward to hearing from you again.
Wir würden uns sehr freuen, von Ihnen bald wieder etwas zu hören.

Formulae – how to express in words

x^0	x to the power of zero
x^1	x to the power of one
x^{-1}	x to the power of minus one
x^{-2}	x to the power of minus two
x^2	x squared
x^3	x cubed
x^4	x to the fourth
$\sqrt[2]{x}$	square root of x
$\sqrt[3]{x}$	cube root of x
$\sqrt[4]{x}$	fourth root of x
$(a+b)^2$	a plus b all squared
	(*or:* a plus b in brackets squared)

$R_t = \dfrac{u_t U^2 10^4}{S_n}$ — (Capital) R sub small t equals (small) u sub t times (capital) U squared times 10 to the fourth, all over (capital) S sub small n

$\dfrac{dy}{dx}$ — dy by dx

$\displaystyle\int ax\,dx = a\int x\,dx = \dfrac{ax^2}{2} + C$ — Integral of ax dx equals a integral of x dx equals ax squared over two, plus C

$U_K = \dfrac{U_q R_a}{R_i + R_a}$ — (capital) U sub (capital) K equals (capital) U sub (small) q times (capital) R sub (small) a, all over (capital) R sub (small) i plus (capital) R sub (small) a

$R = \dfrac{1}{R_1} + \dfrac{1}{R_2} + \dfrac{1}{R_3}$ — (capital) R equals 1 over (capital) R sub 1, plus 1 over (capital) R sub 2, plus 1 over (capital) R sub 3

$C = 4\pi\varepsilon\,\dfrac{r_1 r_2}{r_2 - r_1}$ — (capital) C equals 4 times π (pi), times ε (epsilon); (now follows fraction bar): (small) r sub 1 times (small) r sub 2, all over (small) r sub 2 minus (small) r sub 1

$\omega = \sqrt{\dfrac{1}{LC} - \left(\dfrac{R}{2L}\right)^2}$ — (small) ω (omega) equals, all following under large square root: 1 over (capital) L, times (capital) C minus, the following all in brackets square root: 1 over (capital) R over 2 times (capital) L

$y = y_0 e^{-\delta t} \sin\varphi$ — (small) y equals (small) y sub 0 (zero) times (small) e to the power of minus (small) δ (delta) times (small) t, times sin (small) φ (phi)

How to pronounce these tricky words

analysis [əˈnæləsis] Analyse
ancillary [ænˈsiləri] Hilfs …, Neben …
armature [ˈɑːmətjuə] Anker (elektr.)
auxiliaries [ɔːgˈziljəris] Hilfsbetriebe
bearing [ˈbɛəriŋ] Lager
cascade [kæsˈkeid] Kaskade
catastrophe [kəˈtæstrəfi] Katastrophe
cathode [ˈkæθoud] Kat(h)ode
centrifugal force [senˈtrifjugəl] Zentrifugalkraft
ceramics [siˈræmiks] Keramik
chaos [ˈkeiɔs] Chaos
circumference [səˈkʌmfərəns] Umkreis, Umfang
cleanliness [ˈklenlinis] Sauberkeit, Reinlichkeit
coefficient [kouiˈfiʃənt] Koeffizient
comment [ˈkɔment] Stellungnahme, Kommentar
comparison [kəmˈpærisn] Vergleich
component [kəmˈpounənt] (Bestand-)Teil
concrete [ˈkɔnkriːt] Beton
console [ˈkɔsoul] Konsole, Pult
crystal [kristl] Kristall
data [ˈdeitə] Daten, Angaben
debris [ˈdebriː] Trümmer, Schutt
deprecation [depriˈkeiʃən] Ablehnung, Mißbilligung
depreciation [dipriːʃiˈeiʃən] Abschreibung, Herabsetzung
detail [ˈdiːteil] Einzelheit
diagram [ˈdaiəgræm] Plan, Schema, Diagramm
discrepancy [disˈkrepənsi] Diskrepanz
discretion [disˈkreʃən] Geschick, Umsicht, Belieben
divergence [daiˈvəːdʒəns] Divergenz, Auseinanderlaufen
electrolyte [iˈlektroulait] Elektrolyt
emphasis [ˈemfəsis] Betonung, Gewicht, Schwerpunkt
example [igˈzɑːmpl] Beispiel
excerpt [ˈeksəːpt] Auszug
executive [igˈzekjutiv] leitender Angestellter, Beamter
exhaust gas [igˈzɔːst gæs] Abgas
facsimile [fækˈsimili] Faksimile, Reproduktion

fatigue limit [fə·tiːg ·limit] Ermüdungsgrenze
filament [·filəmənt] (Glüh-)Faden
floodlight [·flʌdlait] Flutlicht
frequency [·friːkwənsi] Frequenz
galvanometer [gælvə·nɔmitə] Galvanometer
gasometer [gæ·sɔmitə] Gasbehälter
gauge [geidʒ] Eichmaß, Messgerät
goniometer [gouni·ɔmitə] Winkelmesser
hazard [·hæzəd] Gefahr, Risiko
hexagonal bolt [hek·sægənl boult] Sechskantschraube
hydraulics [hai·drɔːliks] Hydraulik
hydrogen [·haidrədʒən] Wasserstoff
hygrometer [hai·grɔmitə] Luftfeuchtemesser
hyperbola [hai·pɜːbələ] Hyperbel
impedance [im·piːdəns] Impedanz
indictment [in·daitmənt] Anklage
incandescent lamp [inkæn·desnt læmp] Glühlampe
increment [·inkrimənt] Zuwachs, Zunahme
instantaneous [instən·teinjəs] Sofort …, Moment …
knowledge [·nɔlidʒ] Wissen, Kenntnisse
laboratory [lə·bɔrət(ə)ri] Laboratorium
legend [·ledʒənd] Legende, erläuternder Text
lever [·liːvə] Hebel
maintenance [·meintinəns] Instandhaltung, Wartung
mercury [·mɜːkjuri] Quecksilber
miscellaneous [misi·leinjəs] Verschiedenes
molybdenum [mə·libdənəm] Molybdän
neutron [·njuːtrɔn] Neutron
nomenclature [nou·menklətʃə] Nomenklatur, Bezeichnungen
oxygen [·ɔksidʒən] Sauerstoff
parabola [pə·ræbələ] Parabel
parameter [pə·ræmitə] Parameter
parentheses [pə·renθisis] (runde) Klammern
personnel [pɜːsə·nel] Personal
phenomenon [fi·nɔminən] Phänomen
pivot [·pivət] Drehpunkt, (Dreh-)Zapfen
porcelain [·pɔːslin] Porzellan
potentiometer [pətenʃi·ɔmitə] Potentiometer
preference [·prefərəns] Vorrang, Vorzug

process [ˈprouses] Prozess
prototype [ˈproutətaip] Prototyp
psychiatrist [saiˈkaiətrist] Psychiater
record [ˈrekɔ:d] Niederschrift, Aufzeichnung
receipt [riˈsi:t] Empfang, Quittung
sample [sɑ:mpl] Muster
schedule brit.: [ˈʃedju:l] am.: [ˈskedʒu:l] Aufstellung, Plan
scheme [ski:m] Schema, Anlage
species [spi:ʃi:z] Art, Spezies
specimen [ˈspesimin] Exemplar, Muster
speedometer [spiˈdɔmitə] Geschwindigkeitsmesser
telegraphy [tiˈlegrəfi] Telegraphie
thread [θred] Gewinde, Faden

Modern English for Mechanical Engineers on Audio CD

Nr. 1:
How to avoid misunderstandings when handling specifications

Even with accurately written specifications, misunderstandings can occur. One means of preventing misreadings is to include key drawings which provide a basis for discussion on specific points.

Building and layout plans can be regarded as key plans, as can also one-line diagrams for electrical systems. It is easier to talk to your counterpart on the telephone about the equipment if both of you have the same plans with comprehensive information in front of you, not just a written text.

Sometimes people call up who have difficulty expressing themselves clearly in English. Plans which contain plenty of detail will help to overcome possible communication problems.

A customer will be impressed if he receives the information he wants without delay.

Furthermore, a detailed question can be answered without having too much paper on the table. It is of great advantage to use scaled-down plans. However, great care must be taken that lettering of suitable size is used. The information on the reduced diagram or sketch might otherwise be illegible.

Georg Möllerke, Engineering Report

to avoid vermeiden
missunderstandings Missverständnisse
to handle umgehen mit, handhaben
specification Bauvorschrift, Pflichtenheft, Spezifikation
even sogar, selbst
accurate(ly) sorgfältig, genau
to prevent vermeiden, verhindern
misreadings falsches Ablesen
to include einbeziehen, einschließen
key drawing Schlüsselplan, Hauptplan
to provide vorsehen, liefern
building and layout plans Gebäude- und Anordnungspläne
to regard betrachten
one-line diagram Übersichtsplan; *auch:* Hauptschaltplan
counterpart Gegenüber; *sonst auch:* Gegenstück
equipment Ausrüstung, Anlage, Gerät(e)
comprehensive umfassend, inhaltsreich
to express sich ausdrücken
to contain enthalten, umfassen
detail Einzelheit

to overcome fertigwerden (mit), bewältigen

communication problems Verständigungsschwierigkeiten

customer Kunde

impressed beeindruckt

to receive erhalten, empfangen

delay Verzögerung

advantage Vorteil

scaled-down verkleinert

lettering Buchstaben(auswahl)

suitable passend, geeignet

size Größe

reduced verkleinert, reduziert

diagram Schaltplan, Diagramm

illegible unleserlich

Nr. 2:
Bedplate and frames of a marine diesel engine

bedplate Grundplatte

frame Ständer

marine diesel engine Schiffsdieselmotor

built (to build) gebaut

structure Konstruktion, Aufbau, Bauart

inclusion Aufnahme, Einschluss

cast steel Guss-Stahl

construction Aufbau; *sonst auch:* Bau

to adopt *hier:* verwenden; *sonst:* annnehmen, adoptieren

to consist of bestehen aus

section Abschnitt, Sektion

to bolt together zusammenschrauben

The bedplates and frames for the largest Fiat engines are normally built as a steel structure, with the inclusion of cast-steel elements. A cast-iron construction is adopted for the smaller engine types.

The bedplate consists of sections that are strongly bolted together. The aftermost section is connected to the thrust-block section, thus providing great rigidity and ensuring complete and easy alignment. The thrust block is lubricated with oil directly drawn from the general lubricating system.

The transverse girders of the bedplate contain the main bearing housings. These are all machined together for obtaining perfect crankshaft alignment. The "A" frames are mounted on the bedplate and support the cylinders.

The "A" frames on one side of the engine are connected to each other by the crosshead guides and, on the other, by simple strut elements. The openings between the frames are closed by large access doors.

Marine Diesel Engines, Butterworth and Heinemann, Jordan Hill, England

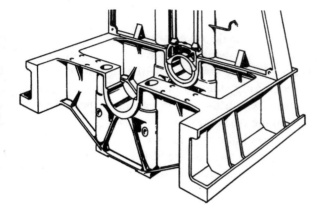

aftermost hinterst

to connect to verbinden mit; *sonst auch:* anschließen an

thrust-block Drucklager; *sonst auch:* Querstück

to provide sichern, vorsehen; *sonst auch:* liefern

rigidity Festigkeit, Steifheit

to ensure sichern, gewährleisten

alignment Ausrichtung, Fluchtung

to lubricate schmieren

to draw entnehmen; *sonst auch:* entziehen

lubricating system Schmieranlage, -system

transverse girder Bindequerträger

to contain enthalten, aufnehmen

main bearing housing Kurbelwellen-Lagerstuhl

to machine together zusammen (d. h. gleichzeitig) maschinell bearbeiten

to obtain erhalten

crankshaft Kurbelwelle

to mount aufbauen, vorsehen, montieren

to support verstärken, abstützen

to connect to each other gegenseitig verbinden

crosshead guide Kreuzkopfführung

strut Strebe, Versteifung

access door Zugangsklappe, Zugangstür

Nr. 3:
Cylinder liner of a marine diesel engine

cylinder liner Zylinderlaufbüchse
marine diesel engine Schiffsdieselmoror
exhaust port Auspuffkanal,
  Austrittsöffnung
scavenging port Spülschlitz,
  Spülluftkanal
water space Wasserraum
to seal abschließen, abdichten
by means of mittels
stuffing box Stopfbüchse
leakage groove Lecknut
in the event of im Falle, falls
visible (-bly) sichtbar
to discharge auslaufen; *sonst
  auch:* entladen
cast iron alloy Gusseisenlegierung
wearing property Laufeigenschaft, Verschleißeigenschaft
proven (to prove) bewährt
manoevring side Manövrierseite (Steuerstand)
inspection hole Schauloch
to provide vorsehen
piston Kolben
to shut down abstellen
to enable ermöglichen, in den
  Stand setzen
B.D.C. bottom dead centre:
  unterer Totpunkt
soot-blower Rußbläser
one-piece in einem Stück
to insert einsetzen
to fasten befestigen
flange Flansch
design Ausführung, Konstruktion

The figure shows a cylinder liner, with exhaust and scavenging ports, in a cylinder block. The water space is sealed by means of a stuffing box, with a leakage groove underneath. In the event of leakage, the water is visibly discharged through this groove.

Liners are made of cast-iron alloy, the wearing properties of which have been proven for many years. In the middle of the cylinder, at the manoeuvring side, an inspection hole is provided through which the piston can be inspected when the engine is shut down.

Inspection holes enable exhaust ports to be cleaned, when the pistons are at B.D.C., with a special tool which is combined with a kind of soot-

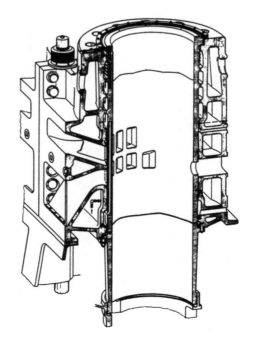

blower. For smaller engines the liner is in one piece, inserted from the top of the cylinder block.

The larger engines have mostly two-piece liners, the lower part being inserted from the bottom end of the cylinder block and fastened to it by a flange. Sometimes, a one-piece liner design is also used for the larger engine types. Both designs have their advantages as regards manufacturing and servicing of the engine.

Marine Diesel engines, Butterworth and Heinemann, Jordan Hill, England

advanatge Vorteil
as regards was betrifft, hinsichtlich
servicing Wartung; *manchmal auch:* Bedienung

That's the trouble nowadays – no knowledge of the classics!

Nr. 4:
Starting a centrifugal pump

A centrifugal feed pump must not be operated unless it is filled with water. This is called priming. The pump casing, the suction pipe and the discharge pipe up to the check valve must be completely filled.

If the water enters the pump suction pipe by gravity, priming is not necessary and the pump will remain full of water when shut down. To fill the pump, open the smaller air-valve on the top of the pump casing until water commences to flow from it, then shut.

If the pump is operated with a suction lift, it may be primed either from an independent water supply or from the discharge line, or by means of a vent connection which will evacuate the pump and suction piping of air.

centrifugal pump Kreiselpumpe
must not *hier:* darf nicht
to operate betreiben, arbeiten
priming Anfüllen
casing Gehäuse
suction pipe Saugleitung, Ansaugrohr
pipe branch Zweigleitung, Abzweigrohr
discharge stop valve Druckabsperrventil
to enter einlaufen, eintreten
gravity Gefälle; *sonst auch:* Schwerkraft, Schwere
to prime anfüllen
necessary notwendig

to remain bleiben
to shut down abstellen
air-valve Luftventil
on the top oben auf
to commence beginnen
suction lift Saughöhe
independent unabhängig
supply Zufluss; *sonst auch:*
  Lieferung, Versorgung
discharge line Entlastungsleitung
by means of mittels
vent connection Entlüftungs-
  anschluß
to evacuate entlüften
check valve Absperrventil
to fit einbauen, einsetzen
case Fall
latter letztere
to proceed vorgehen
lubrication Schmierung

Captions in the pump drawing

1 pump casing and cover
  Pumpengehäuse und
  Gehäusedeckel
2 impeller Laufrad
3 casing ring (bottom)
  Gehäusering (unten)
4 casing ring (top) Gehäusering (oben)
4A locking pins Sperrringe,
  Spannringe
5 pump shaft Pumpenwelle
6 coupling (motor half)
  Kupplung (Motorhälfte)
7 gland Stopfbuchse
8 packing Packung
9 lantern ring (split) Laternenring (zweiteilig,
  geschnitten)
10 neck bush Halsbuchse

The check valve must, of course, be fitted in these cases. The discharge valve and air-valves should be kept closed during the priming of the pump if the latter methods are used. To start the centrifugal pump, proceed as follows:

Check lubrication, and see that pump glands are properly packed and adjusted. Open steam and exhaust casing drain cocks of the driving engine, open steam and exhaust valves; open suction valves and air-cocks. Open turbine throttle valve sufficiently to free the pipelines, steam chest and exhaust casing of water while running turbine at a very low speed. When free of water close the drain cocks and bring the unit up to speed.

Marine Engineering, Butterworth and Heinemann, Jordan Hill, England

Fortsetzung S. 69

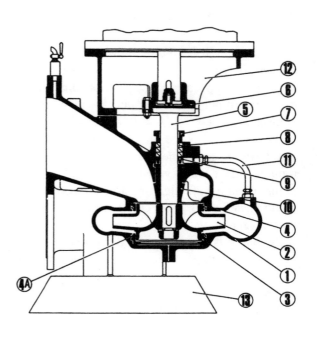

My Sahara-Crossing Slimming holidays are a huge success. Package tours without food, drink or accommodation are available from SFr. 5000 a week.

gland Stoppbüchse
proper(ly) ordnungsgemäß
to pack abdichten, verpacken
to adjust einstellen, ausrichten
exhaust Ausgangs…, Austritts…
drain cock Entleerungshahn
driving engine Antriebsmaschine
throttle valve Drosselventil, Reglerventil
sufficient(ly) ausreichend
steam chest Ventilkasten
speed *hier:* Drehzahl
to bring up to speed hochfahren (auf Nenndrehzahl)

Nr. 5:
Circuit diagram showing principle of automatic swivelling of deburring device for a milling machine

On reaching the feed limit position, limit switch b31 is activated. Thereupon the feed reverses, allowing the limit switch to return to its normal position.
The resulting voltage pulse energizes time-lag relay d1. Contacts d1-3/4 close instantaneously, energizing solenoid valve s1 which causes the deburring device (not shown) to swivel in.
After a preset period elapses, contacts d1-3/4 open, solenoid valve d1 de-energizes and the deburring device swivels out.

circuit diagram Stromlaufplan
principle Prinzip
swivelling Schwenken; **to swivel** *sonst auch:* drehen
deburring device Entgratungsvorrichtung; **device** *sonst auch:* Gerät
milling machine Fräsmaschine
on reaching beim (*oder:* mit) Erreichen
feed limit position Ende (*oder:* Endstellung) des Vorschubs
limit switch Endschalter
to activate betätigen
to reverse umkehren
to allow gestatten
resulting sich (hieraus)

voltage pulse Spannungsimpuls
to energize erregen (Relais),
betätigen, anreizen
time-lag relay Zeitrelais
instantaneous(ly) augenblicklich, sofort
solenoid valve Magnetventil
to cause veranlassen, bewirken; *sonst auch:* verursachen
to swivel in einschwenken
preset vorher eingestellt
period Zeit(raum)
to elapse verstreichen
to de-energize zum Abfall
bringen, entregen
to swivel out zurückschwenken, ausschwenken

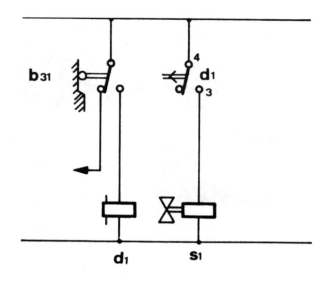

Nr. 6:
Faulty control equipment

First of all, we must remove the top cover.
Als erstes müssen wir die obere Abdeckung
(*oder:* den Deckel) entfernen (*oder:* abnehmen).

Then we must remove the rear plate.
Dann müssen wir die hintere Platte abnehmen.

**Now I'm going to draw out the printed-circuit
board.**
Jetzt werde ich Leiterplatte herausziehen.

Just order your own book catalo-
gue from Carl Hanser Verlag

I'm disconnecting the feeder cable now.
Nun werde ich das Speisekabel abklemmen
(*oder:* lösen, entfernen).

Both current transformers must also be removed.
Beide Stromwandler müssen auch ausgebaut
(*oder:* herausgenommen, entfernt) werden.

The terminal block must be unscrewed.
Der Klemmblock ist abzuschrauben.

The second diode is defective.
Die zweite Diode ist defekt.

Hand me the small screw-driver, please.
Reich' mir bitte den kleinen Schraubenzieher.

I'm now removing the diode.
Ich nehme jetzt die Diode heraus.

We needn't strip down the whole device.
Wir brauchen nicht das ganze Gerät auseinander-
zunehmen.

Would you please check the diode?
Würdest du bitte die Dioden prüfen?

Is there a spare diode?
Ist da (noch) eine Reservediode?

I'm afraid, there's no spare diode.
Ich fürchte, da ist keine Reservediode (mehr).

**Don't worry, Metroniks stock this type of
diode.**
Keine Bange, Metroniks hat diesen Diodentyp auf
Lager.

**Before we continue the controller should be
cleaned.**
Ehe wir weitermachen, sollte das Steuergerät
(*oder:* der Controller) gereinigt werden.

Nr. 7:
Starting up the motors of an automatic bar machine

starting up Anlauf, Starten, Hochfahren
automatic bar machine Stangenautomat
to press drücken
push-button Druckknopf
circuit pressure Druck im Kreislauf; **circuit** *sonst auch:* Stromkreis, Schaltkreis, Schaltung
to reach erreichen
p.s.i.g.: pounds per square inch gauged Pfund pro Quadratzoll gemessen
pressure switch Druckschalter
to illuminate aufleuchten
to release freigeben
interlock Verriegelung
clogged verstopft
main motor Hauptmotor
turret Revolver(kopf)
cross slide Querschlitten
rapid traverse Eilgang, Schnelldurchlauf
proper ordnungsgemäß
condition Bedingung, Zustand

On pressing push-button b1, pump motor m2 will start up. When the circuit pressure has reached 100 p.s.i.g., a pressure switch will illuminate the button b1 and release the interlock which will start the main motor m1.

If the filter becomes clogged, the push-button will not illuminate. The main motor, turret and cross slide rapid traverse will not run up until the pump motor is running under proper conditions.

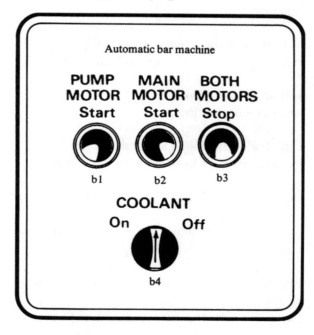

Nr. 8:
Drilling holes in plastics

Accurate drilling or cutting through a flexible plastics tube is wellnigh impossible because plastics tend to stretch under strain.

But accurately worked tubes are often required, for example, as a ball cage in a bearing. Teleflex Inc., of Pennsylvania, proposes a classical simple solution to the problem.

The tube is temporarily frozen hard by feeding it through a jacket kept at low temperature by a refrigerant such as solidified carbon dioxide. Water is then pumped through the tube and this freezes to provide a temporary solid core. Now the drilling can easily be made.

New Scientist, London

to drill bohren
hole Loch, Bohrung
accurate genau, präzise
tube (*or:* **pipe**) Rohr, Leitung
wellnigh fast, so gut wie
to tend neigen
to stretch sich dehnen, ausweiten
strain Belastung, Spannung
required benötigt, erforderlich
ball cage Kugelkäfig
bearing Lager
to propose vorschlagen; *sonst auch:* planen
solution Lösung
temporary (-rily) zeitweise, vorübergehend
frozen (to freeze) gefroren
to feed *hier:* einleiten, einführen; *sonst auch:* speisen
jacket Ummantelung, Hülle
refrigerant Gefriermittel
solidified carbon dioxide CO_2-Eis
to provide vorsehen, liefern
solid core fester Kern
easy (-sily) einfach, leicht

There's nothing like surfing on the Web

Nr. 9:
Calling for the machine tool expert

Starting a telephone call one should say, after greeting, the name, followed by the company name and place.
Example
Good morning. This is (Mr.) Erismann, Kaegi Metalworking Company, speaking from Zollikofen, Switzerland.
If you have to repeat, go on like this: My name is Erismann, Kaegi Metalworking Company ...

Forthcoming:
Growing demand for experts in the
fields of electrical and mechanical
engineering

**Good morning. My name is Erismann, Kaegi
Company, speaking from Zollikofen.**
Guten Morgen. Mein Name ist Erismann, Firma
Kaegi, in Zollikofen.

**I'd like to speak to Mr. Westhouse, your
machine tool expert.**
Ich möchte gern mit Herrn Westhouse sprechen,
Ihrem Werkzeugmaschinen-Fachmann.

**Just a moment. I'll see if Mr. Westhouse is
available.**
Einen Moment. Ich werde mal nachsehen, ob
Herr Westhouse da ist.

**Mr. Westhouse, a Mr. Erismann is on the line
for you.**
Herr Westhouse, ein Herr Erismann möchte Sie
am Telefon sprechen.

Put him through please.
Stellen Sie ihn bitte durch.

Mr. Erismann, I'm putting you through now.
Herr Westhouse, ich stelle Sie jetzt durch.

Hold the line please.
Bleiben Sie bitte am Apparat.

After completing the call:

Please give my regards to Mr. Wilson (*or:*
remember me to Mr. Wilson; *or:* please extend
my greetings to Mr. Wilson).
Bestellen Sie Herrn Wilson eine schönen Gruß.

Goodbye, Mr. Erismann. Thanks for calling.
Auf Wiedersehen, Herr Erismann. Vielen Dank
für den Anruf.

Nr. 10:
A powerful hand ratchet

Ingersoll-Rand company of Woocliff Lake, N.Y., has introduced a new ratchet wrench that combines the extra muscle of a power tool with the portable flexibility of a hand tool.

Unlike other power-driven ratchet wrenches, which need to be connected to compressed-air or electrical lines, the Redi-Ratchet has a self-contained rechargeable battery.

The manufacturer says that this handy and versatile new power tool is rugged enough for use anywhere that small or medium-size bolts, nuts and screws are used: in automotive repair shops and airline maintenance hangars, factories; even around the home garage or workshop.

The Redi-Ratchet weighs only four pounds, measures 14 inches long, has 3/8-inch drive, and is nearly as convenient for professional mechanics to take along as a conventional hand ratchet wrench.

The Engineer, London

powerful leistungsstark
hand ratchet Handratsche, Handknarre; ratchet *auch:* Sperrklinke
to introduce einführen
to combine vereinigen, kombinieren
extra muscle Zusatzkraft, -muskel
power tool Elektrowerkzeug
power-driven elektrisch betrieben
compressed-air line Druckluftleitung
self-contained unabhängig
rechargeable aufladbar
handy handlich, praktisch
versatile vielseitig verwendbar
rugged robust
medium-size mittelgroß
bolt Schraube, Bolzen
nut (Schrauben-)Mutter
screw Schraube
maintenance Wartungs…
to weigh wiegen, wägen
to measure *hier:* Abmessungen aufweisen von
convenient bequem

Brilliant people at the MingProg Secret Service Division in Pulham Down are proud to show their latest major achievements.

Nr. 11:
Throttling case

throttling Gasgeben,
  Beschleunigen
gadget kleines Gerät, Spielzeug
to appeal to Anklang, Gefallen
  finden an
to appal erschrecken, entsetzen
adult Erwachsener
aim Ziel
handle bar grip Lenkstangengriff
sleeve Hülse; *sonst:* Ärmel
gears Zahnräder
fly-wheel Schwungrad
gunning Aufdrehen, Aufheulen, Gas geben

The Ideal Toy Corporation of New York now has a British patent (BP 1 568 176) on a gadget which will appeal to young children as much as it will appal adults hoping for a quiet life.

The aim is to enable child cyclists to make as much noise as a Hell's Angle. According to the patent, a cycle handle bar grip is formed from inner and outer sleeves, like the throttle control of a motor bike. A system of internal gears and clutches rotates a heavy fly-wheel when a child twists the outer sleeve handle like a motor cyclist 'gunning' the engine.

As the fly-wheel rotates, it drags a striker over the metal tip of a resonant diaphragm which looks like a loudspeaker. The result is a series of noises 'closely simulating' those of a motor bike's engine.

The Engineer, London

Nr. 12.
Kenneth Benton, a machine tool expert

series Serie, Reihe
to depict veranschaulichen,
  schildern
event Ereignis, Vorfall
section head Gruppenleiter
engineering company technischer Betrieb, technisches
  Unternehmen
based in mit dem Hauptsitz in
fluid Flüssigkeit
colleague Kollegin, Kollege
note Notiz(zettel)
to receive erhalten

This is a series depicting events in the working life of Kenneth Benton, a section head with Carlisle & Westmore Ltd., a large engineering company based in Birkenhead.

Episode 1.
A new hydraulic fluid for machine tools

Kenneth Benton, his assistant Ellen Parker and their colleague Bruce Boysen discuss the use of a new hydraulic fluid, to be tested for machine tools.

Ellen

Oh, by the way, have you seen the note on your desk?

Kenneth

No, what note? Oh yes, here it is. Bruce is coming in to see us at 10 o'clock. Mmm, that's any minute now.

Ellen

Yes, he wants to show us the specification for a new type of hydraulic fluid for machine tools.

Kenneth

That's right. I remember he mentioned it a while ago, a new hydraulic fluid based on water.

Ellen

Come in.

Bruce

Morning, Ellen. Morning, Kenneth.

Kenneth

Morning, Bruce.

Bruce

I've just received the fluid specification. The product's called Plurasafe. Shall I read you the introduction?

Kenneth

Yes, please, go ahead.

Bruce

Hydraulic fluids are the bloodstream of heavy industry. The automative, steelmaking, mining and machine tool industries require hundreds of millions of gallons a year, and up to 90 per cent of these fluids are petroleum-based.

introduction Einleitung, Einführung
to go ahead weitermachen
bloodstream Blutkreislauf
heavy industry Schwerindustrie
to require benötigen
to develop entwickeln
subsidiary Tochtergesellschaft
at present momentan, jetzt
description Beschreibung
to possess besitzen
lubricating property Schmiereigenschaft
appropriate ordnungsgemäß
operating pressure Betriebsdruck
to apply anwenden, verwenden
square inch Quadratzoll
development Entwicklung

Sometimes no easy job, when everybody wants your advice and help. And they look at you, for they know you'll struggle for a solution. And your own help: Technical literature from Carl Hanser Verlag.

There's nothing like the electronic work simulator from the Ministry of Progress.

A new type of hydraulic fluid has now been developed by the BASF Wyandotte Corporation, an American subsidiary of the West German chemical manufacturer based in Ludwigshafen.

Plurasafe fluids, as they are called, are said to be the first water-based fluids capable of covering most of the industrial requirements currently met by petroleum-based liquids.

Ellen
Sounds promising, any mention of costs?

Bruce
Hm, ah yes. The price will be around $1.20 per gallon.

Kenneth
Oh, well, I believe we're paying $2.10 a gallon at present. How does the description go on, Bruce?

Bruce
It says: These fluids possess the high viscosity and lubricating properties appropriate to the operation of heavy machinery.

Ellen
And do they give the operating pressure?

Bruce
Let's see. Yes, here we are: They can be applied for pressures up to 1,000 pounds per square inch and they are much safer than petroleum-based fluids.

Kenneth
You know, I think we should go up and see our managing director. I'd like to hear what Mr. Aubrey has to say about this development.

Nr. 13:
Episode 2. New TM lathe being prepared for tests

Bruce Boysen of the development department explains the new CNC toolmaker's lathe to Kenneth Benton and Ellen Parker.

Ellen
So this is the new prototype lathe you wanted to show us? This toolmaker's lathe?

Bruce
Yes, this is it, our TM2 model. As you can see, it's based on the TM1 lathe, but includes some innovations, and the performance has been considerably improved.

Kenneth
Mainly the cutting speed, I suppose?

Bruce
That's right, especially the cutting speed. Let me put it like this: there's an enormous reduction of machining time, which means lower costs.

Ellen
We could compare some performance data with our old TM1 lathe, couldn't we?

Bruce
Certainly. But look, I've prepared this lathe to machine a spigot 40 mm in diameter, 48 mm long. You can time it yourself.

Ellen
All right. You can start now!

development department Entwicklungs-Abteilung
to explain erläutern, erklären
toolmaker's lathe (TM lathe) Drehmaschine für Werkzeugmacherei und Vorrichtungsbau
to base on basieren auf
to include einschließen
innovations Neuerungen
performance Leistung, Leistungsvermögen
considerably beträchtlich
to improve verbessern
cutting speed Schnittgeschwindigkeit
to suppose annehmen, vermuten
to put it *hier:* es so ausdrücken
machining time Bearbeitungszeit, Grundzeit
to compare vergleichen
to machine bearbeiten (maschinell)
spigot (Dreh-)Zapfen; *auch:* Zentriersatz
diameter Durchmesser
feed rate Vorschubgeschwindigkeit
revolution Umdrehung
quiet ruhig, geräuscharm
to admit zugeben, zugestehen
improvement Verbesserung
sales potential Vertriebspotential
sophisticated hochentwickelt, äußerst leistungsfähig

prospective möglich(e)
customer Kunde
efficiency Leistungsfähigkeit,
  Leistungsvermögen

Communication problems.

Bruce
The speed is 590 ft. per minute, the feed rate 0.008 in. per revolution.

Kenneth
Very quiet running, and excellent work.

Ellen
Well, Bruce, I must admit the new model is a great improvement on the TM1, that would seem to be 25 per cent less machining time. Congratulations.

Kenneth
Tell me, Bruce, what's the sales potential for this sophisticated lathe?

Bruce
Well, there's no other machine like this in England. It's only in Switzerland that you'll find a similar machine. And there are already five prospective customers. Efficiency counts, you see.

Nr. 14:
Episode 3. Preparing for a business trip

to prepare vorbereiten
business trip Geschäftsreise
central figure Schlüsselfigur,
  zentrale Figur
to summon herbeirufen, herbestellen
to request ersuchen, bitten
fault Fehler, Störung
arisen (to arise) aufgetreten
machining centre Bearbei-
  tungszentrum
to investigate untersuchen,
  nachspüren

Kenneth Benton, the central figure of this series, is summoned by the managing director, Ben Aubrey. He is requested to go on a business trip to Gloucester. A fault has arisen in the maching centre of Delta Instruments Limited and Kenneth is to investigate the cause. He is also to pay a visit to Brian Sandham, the chief manufacturing engineer.

Colleague
Hold on, he's just coming now. Kenneth you've arrived just in time. You're wanted on the telephone.

Kenneth
Hello, Benton here.

Alice
Good morning, Kenneth. This is Alice speaking.
Would you please come up to Ben? He wants to
see you as soon as possible.

Kenneth
All right, Alice. I'll come up immediately.

Ben
Ah, Kenneth. Do sit down. There's a special mission for you, Delta Instruments in Gloucester
again. Could you go there the day after tomor-
row?

Kenneth
Hmm. One day later would suit me better. The
test for the Vermont milling machines ought to be
completed beforehand.

Ben
Oh yes, of course. I nearly forgot.

Kenneth
I'm rather puzzled, though. The Delta plant has
been operating satisfactorily for six months now.

Ben
Generally speaking, yes. But there's one NC turret-type lathe that's not giving full performance.

Kenneth
Do you know more about the trouble there.

Ben
Sorry, Kenneth. I've no details on this matter.

cause Ursache
to pay a visit Besuch abstatten
chief manufacturing
  engineer Leiter der Produktion
hold on bleib dran
to arrive eintreffen, ankommen
immediately sofort, unverzüglich
to suit passen, recht sein
milling machine Fräsmaschine
ought to be sollten sein
completed fertig(gestellt)
beforehand vorher
puzzled überrascht, verwirrt
plant Anlage
turret-type lathe Revolverdrehmaschine
performance Leistung, Leistungsvermögen
to impress beeindrucken
to look after sich kümmern
equipment Gerät(e), Ausrüstung, Anlage(n)
commissioning (offizielle)
  Inbetriebsetzung, Übergabe
order Bestellung, Auftrag
at least mindestens, wenigstens
automatic screw machine
  Schraubenautomat

"I just met the most incredible aluminium sliding salesman …"

Kenneth
Don't you think our people could solve this problem?

Ben
Yes, they certainly could. But I'd like you to pay a visit to Brian Sandham, the chief manufacturing engineer.

Kenneth
Ah, I see the point.

Ben
It will impress them to see how well we're looking after the equipment so long after commissioning.

Kenneth
So it's really a goodwill tour?

Ben
Indeed it is. What's more, we're hoping to receive a further order from them by December of next year, at least ten automatic screw machines.

Nr. 15:
Episode 4. Investigations in the Gloucester plant

investigation Untersuchung, Nachforschung
plant Anlage, Fabrik
fault Fehler, Defekt
turret lathe Revolverdreh-maschine
flaw Fehler; *sonst auch:* Riss, Bruch
winding Wicklung
to expect erwarten

Kenneth Benton meets Brian Sandham, chief manufacturing engineer of Delta Instruments Limited. Kenneth quickly finds the fault in the NC turret-type lathe: an electric motor with a flaw in the winding.

Kenneth
Good morning.

Reception
Good morning, Sir. What can I do for you?

Kenneth
I'd like to see Mr. Sandham, the chief manufacturing engineer.

Reception
Oh yes. We've been expecting you. I'd take you up to see Mr. Sandham straight away.
Would you come this way, please? His office is on the second floor...
Here we are. It's Mr. Benton of Carlisle and Westmore.

Sandham
Hello, Mr. Benton. How are you? Nice to see you again.

Kenneth
Fine, thanks. And how are you, Mr. Sandham?

Sandham
I'm fine, too. Things are coming along well here.
(After some talk.) And now let's have a look at number eight turret lathe, it's not working at full capacity. I'm sure you'll soon find out what's wrong.

Kenneth
I hope so.

Sandham
This is the turret that's giving us a bit of trouble.

Kenneth
(After some turret checking.)
The fault is not in the electronic equipment. It's the electric motor. Have a look at the ohmmeter. The windings clearly indicate a fault.

---

to **announce** ankündigen
things are coming along well
  etwa: bei uns läuft alles ganz gut
capacity Leistung, Kapazität
to **enter** betreten, eintreten
to **indicate** anzeigen
spare motor Reservemotor
in stock auf Lager
to **restore** wieder in Ordnung bringen

Sandham
Do you have spare motors in stock?

Kenneth
Oh, certainly, Mr. Sandham. It'll only take us a day to restore your turret.

Nr. 16:
Episode 5. Introducing a junior engineer

to introduce einführen, vorstellen
junior engineer junger Ingenieur
to return zurückkehren
experiences Erfahrungen; *sonst auch:* Erlebnisse
to appear erscheinen
I could do with one ich könnte eine (Tasse Kaffee) gebrauchen
primarily hauptsächlich
designer Konstrukteur
milling machine Fräsmaschine
field (Fach-)Gebiet
development group Entwicklungsgruppe
sales department Vertriebsabteilung
sophisticated hochentwickelt, fortgeschritten
to lead führen
recent(ly) kürzlich
progress Fortschritt
to develop entwickeln
if my memory serves me right wenn ich mich recht erinnere
Polytechnic Technische Universität
to recommend empfehlen
lecturer Dozent

Kenneth Benton has just returned from his trip to Delta Instruments in Gloucester. He has been talking about his experiences there to Ben Aubrey, the director. Now he has to see to introducing a new engineer.

Kenneth
Do you need me any longer? I've got to go and look after our new engineer. Charles Milton.

Ben
Yes, of course, introduce him around and so on. Off you go, then.

Kenneth
Well, now that we've introduced ourselves, how about a cup of coffee?

Charles
Yes, please. I could do with one.

Kenneth
You're primarily a designer of milling machines, aren't you, Mr. Milton.

Charles
Well, I've been in this field for three years. Last year I worked in the NC development group of Kendall and Biggs.

Kenneth

Ah well, you've come to the right place, then.

Charles

I think so, too.

Kenneth

In our sales department, we specialize in turret-type machines as well as milling machines. All equipment with sophisticated numerical controls.

Charles

As far as I know, this company leads the field in turret lathes. But I read in 'Metalworking Production' quite recently that you're making great progress in developing toolmaker's lathes.

Kenneth

That's right. In a year's time, we'll be marketing a new line in small lathes.

Charles

I see.

Kenneth

If my memory serves me right, you were at the London Polytechnic, weren't you?

Charles

That's right. I left there four years ago.

Kenneth

By the way, you were recommended to us by a lecturer at the Polytechnic: Professor Wilson.

Nr. 17:
Episode 6. A badly needed contract

badly needed dringend benötigt
contract Auftrag, Kontrakt
to award zuerkennen, gewinnen
delivery Lieferung
automatic screw machine Schraubenautomat
to die was cast die Würfel sind gefallen: *wörtlich:* der Würfel war gefallen
equipment Ausrüstung
surprise Überraschung
to consider bedenken, erwägen
genuine echt
competitor Konkurrent
essential wesentlich
major wichtigst, Haupt…
order *hier:* Größenordnung
to comprise umfassen
relief Erleichterung
not at full stretch nicht voll ausgelastet
to doubt Zweifel hegen
component Einzelteil
to obtain erhalten
schedule Plan, Aufstellung

The firm of Carlisle and Westmore Limited has been awarded the contract for the delivery and installation of ten automatic screw machines.

Ellen

A few minutes ago there was a telephone call from Frank. He said the die was cast, we've got the order from Delta Instruments in Gloucester.

Kenneth

For eight machines?

Ellen

For all ten automatic screw machines!

Kenneth

How about the electronic equipment?

Ellen

I understand the electronic equipment is included.

Kenneth

Well, that really is a surprise, considering there were four 'genuine' competitors.

Ellen

Frank thought we had a good chance right from the start. After all, we were able to meet all essential points of the specification, and the major equipment had to be from one manufacturer.

Kenneth

That's right. And a contract of this order, around one million pounds, is just what we needed.

Ellen

Ellen Parker. Yes, quite correct, Henry we've got that Delta order. Yes, for the whole plant, comprising ten machines – as well as the electronic equipment. I bet you are! He's relieved.

Kenneth

Well, I can understand his relief. His group hasn't been working at full stretch for some weeks.

Ellen

We'll have to arrange some extra meetings. We haven't had a contract of this size for two years.

Kenneth

That's true.

Ellen

And I very much doubt if the components can be obtained in the schedule given.

Kenneth

That's just the problem. Well, I must get off to my appointment now. I'll see you later, Ellen.

Novel food tests are being performed at the Ministry of Progress, Pulham Down.

Dictionary

A

a.m. (Lat.) ante meridiem: before noon

able imstande; *auch:* fähig

abrasive Schleif..., Schmirgel...

access door Zugangsklappe, Zugangstür

access Zugang, Zutritt

accident Unfall

accuracy Genauigkeit, Präzision

accurate genau, präzise

accurate(ly) sorgfältig, genau

achievement Leistung, Errungenschaft

across *hier:* im Durchmesser

actual(ly) tatsächlich

adequate ausreichend, genügend

adult erwachsener

advanced hochentwickelt, fortgeschritten

advantage Vorteil

advice Ratschlag, Hinweis

affiliation Zugehörigkeit

aftermost hinterst

ahead of his time seiner Zeit voraus

aim Ziel

aimed at abzielend auf, absehend auf

air-freight capacity Luftfracht, Aufnahmevermögen

air-valve Luftventil

alerted auf der Hut, alarmiert; *sonst auch:* aufgeweckt

alignment Ausrichtung, Fluchtung

all-purpose machine Allzweckmaschine

allowance for depreciation Billigung zur Abschreibung

ambitious ehrgeizig, anspruchsvoll

amphibious vehicle Amphibien-Fahrzeug

ancient alt, altertümlich

anniversary Jahrestag, jährlicher Gedenktag

annual jährlich, Jahres...

appliance (Haushalts-)Gerät

appointment Verabredung, Termin

appropriate ordnungsgemäß
area Fläche, Gebiet
arisen (to arise) aufgetreten
array (im Namen) Anordnung, Reihe
arrest rates Anzahl der Festnahmen
artificial künstlich
as regards was betrifft, hinsichtlich
at least mindestens, wenigstens
at present momentan, jetzig
attempt Versuch
attendant Aufseher
authority Verwaltung, Behörde
automatic bar machine Stangenautomat
automatic screw machine Schraubenautomat
auxiliary diesel generator set Hilfs-D/G-Aggregat
available verfügbar, vorhanden
average Durchschnitt
avionics Elektronik der Luftfahrt

B
B.D.C. bottom dead centre: unterer Totpunkt
baby boomers Menschen aus starken Geburtsjahrgängen
badly needed dringend benötigt
baffled verwirrt, verblüfft
baggage area Gepäckbereich
ball cage Kugelkäfig
barrister Anwalt
based in mit dem Hauptsitz in
bearing Lager
bedplate Grundplatte
bedroom furniture Schlafzimmermöbel
beforehand vorher
belt Gürtel
beneficial förderlich, nutzbringend
bike ridership Gemeinschaft der Radfahrer
bin bag Behältertasche
bloodstream Blutkreislauf
bolt Schraube, Bolzen
boon Segen, Wohltat, Gefälligkeit

bound to rules an Vorschriften gebunden
brain Gehirn
brass-and-teak aus Messing und Teakholz bestehend
breathtaking atemberaubend
building and layout plans Gebäude- und Anordnungspläne
built (to build) gebaut
built-in eingebaut
bulb "Glühbirne," Glühlampe
business trip Geschäftsreise
by means of mittels
by the time *hier:* bis er soweit ist
by-product Nebenprodukt

C

calculating machine Rechenmaschine, Rechner
calculation aids Rechnungshilfen
call office Fernsprechbüro
caller Anrufer
camshaft Nockenwelle
capable imstande, fähig
capacity Leistung, Kapazität
car engine Automotor
carbon dioxide Kohlenstoffdioxid
carbon Kohlenstoff
cardboard Pappe
career guidance Richtlinien für eine Karriere
case Fall
casing Gehäuse
casing ring (bottom) Gehäusering (unten)
casing ring (top) Gehäusering (oben)
cast iron alloy Gusseisenlegierung
cast steel Guss-Stahl
casual nicht auffällig, salopp, sportlich
catalytic converter Katalysator
cause Ursache
central figure Schlüsselfigur, zentrale Figur
centrifugal pump Kreiselpumpe
CEO chief executive officer; *etwa:* Generaldirektor
chairman Vorsitzender

charged aufgeladen
chat room "Treff-"Lokal, Raum für Plaudereien
check valve Absperrventil
chief executive *etwa:* Generaldirektor
chief manufacturing engineer Leiter der Produktion
chip elektronischer Baustein, Plättchen, Chip
chose (to choose) wählte
circuit diagram Stromlaufplan
circuit pressure Druck im Kreislauf; **circuit** *sonst auch:* Stromkreis,
    Schaltkreis, Schaltung
circumstances Bedingungen, Umstände
citizen Staatsbürger
claim Bekanntgabe; *auch:* Behauptung, Anspruch
clandestine(ly) heimlich, versteckt
class reunion Klassentreffen, -zusammenkunft; **reunion** *auch:* Versöhnung,
    Wiedervereinigung
clogged verstopft
coating Schicht, Überzug
colleague Kollegin, Kollege
column Kolumne, Spalte
combustible brennbar
combustion Verbrennung
command *hier:* Beherrschen
Commander-in-Chief Oberbefehlshaber
commissioning (offizielle) Inbetriebsetzung, Übergabe
common consciousness allgemeines Bewusstsein
common sight gewohnter Anblick
commonplace alltäglich
communication problems Verständigungsschwierigkeiten
comparable vergleichbar
competitor Konkurrent
completed fertig(gestellt)
component Bauteil, Einzelteil, Komponente
comprehensive umfassend, inhaltsreich
compressed-air line Druckluftleitung
computer in charge der zugeschaltete (*oder:* zuständige) Computer; **in charge**
    sonst: unter Leitung, betraut
concern Besorgnis, Sorge
concerning betreffend

condition Bedingung, Zustand
confused verwirrt, irritiert
connecting rod Pleuelstange
considerable (-bly) beträchtlich
consideration Betrachtung, Überlegung
construction Aufbau; *sonst auch:* Bau, *hier:* Bauindustrie
contract Auftrag, Kontrakt
controlled gesteuert
convenient bequem
conversion *hier:* Umbau; *sonst:* Umwandlung, Verwandlung
corporate betreffend eines Unternehmens, *sonst auch:* Körperschafts…
corporate recruiting Anwerbung durch Firmen
counter Schalter
counterpart Gegenüber; *sonst auch:* Gegenstück
coupling (motor half) Kupplung (Motorhälfte)
coveted reminder begehrtes Erinnerungsstück
crack plant Crackanlage, 'Spaltanlage'
craft Luftschiff, Flugzeug, Raumfahrzeug oder Fahrzeug allgemein
crammed vollgestopft, dichtgedrängt
crankcase Kurbelwanne
crankshaft Kurbelwelle
cross slide Querschlitten
crosshead guide Kreuzkopfführung
crossing Überfahrt, Überquerung
crucial entscheidend, wichtig
cruise at fliegen in … Höhe
cruise circuit Kreuzfahrtroute; **circuit** *auch für:* Stromkreis, Wasserkreis, Kreislauf
cruise liner Passagierschiff, Kreuzfahrtschiff
cruise speed Reisegeschwindigkeit, Marschfahrt
cruise vessel Kreuzfahrtschiff *auch:* **cruise liner** Kreuzfahrtschiff
cruising event Ereignis bei einer Kreuzfahrt
crushed zerstoßen, zerdrückt
curious neugierig
current momentan, jetzig
current Strom
custom Brauch, Gewohnheit
customer Kunde
customs 1. Gewohnheiten, 2. Zoll(ämter)

cutting edge Schneidkante
cutting speed Schnittgeschwindigkeit
cylinder head Zylinderkopf
cylinder liner Zylinderlaufbüchse

D
deadline letzter Termin, Fristablauf
deadly sins Todsünden
deburring device Entgratungsvorrichtung; **device** *sonst auch:* Gerät
decade Jahrzehnt
decent anständig, schicklich
decisive entscheidend
decline Niedergang, Rückfall, Rückgang
delay Verzögerung
delighted begeistert, 'entzückt'
delivery Lieferung
delivery van Lieferwagen
demand Nachfrage, Bedarf; *sonst auch:* Forderung
demise Ableben; *sonst auch:* Besitzübertragung
Department of Energy Ministerium für Energieerzeugung
dependent on abhängig von
deposition Ablagerung
description Beschreibung
design Ausführung, Konstruktion
design designer Konstrukteur
desktop computer Tischcomputer
destination Zielort
detail Einzelheit
development department Entwicklungs-Abteilung
development Entwicklung
development group Entwicklungsgruppe
device Gerät, Apparatur
diagram Schaltplan, Diagramm
diameter Durchmesser
diamond Diamant
diesel engine Dieselmotor; *im Englischen nicht:* 'diesel motor'
direct injection Direkteinspritzung
disadvantage Nachteil
disc-shaped scheibenförmig

discharge line Entlastungsleitung
discharge stop valve Druckabsperrventil
discretion Umsicht, Besonnenheit
distinguished geehrt, verdient
does not insist on besteht nicht darauf
dominance Vorherrschaft, Dominanz
drain cock Entleerungshahn
driving engine Antriebsmaschine
dubbing Synchronisieren
dubious(ly) zweifelnd; *sonst auch:* fragwürdig, unbestimmt
dud *hier:* platt; *sonst:* Reinfall
duties *hier:* Abgaben
dwelling place Wohnung, Wohnsitz

E
each rated at jeder mit einer (Nenn-)Leistung von
easy (-sily) einfach, leicht
economical wirtschaftlich
economy Wirtschaft(lichkeit)
educative erzieherisch; *sonst:* sich bildend
effectiveness Wirkung; *auch:* Leistungsvermögen, Effektivität
efficiency Leistungsfähigkeit, Leistungsvermögen
efficient leistungsfähig, effektiv
efficient(ly) wirksam, effizient
effort Anstrengung, Bemühen
electrician Elektriker
electricity bill Stromrechnung
electricity board Elektrizitätsbehörde
electricity generation Elektrizitätserzeugung
embassy Botschaft
emergency generator set Notstromaggregat
encouragement Ermutigung
end of the line Ende der Möglichkeiten, Ende der Leitung
energy content Energiegehalt
energy source Energiequelle
energy-efficient energiesparend
engine (Diesel-)Motor, (Verbrennungs-)Motor; *sonst auch:* Triebwerk
engine exhausts *hier:* Abgase von Dieselmotoren
engine fuel Treibstoff für Motoren; *hier gemeint:* Otto- und Dieselmotoren

engine option Auswahl des Motors
engineering company technischer Betrieb, technisches Unternehmen
engineering education technische Ausbildung
engineering feat technische Großtat; **feat** *auch:* Meisterstück, Kraftakt
engineering profession der Beruf des Ingenieurs
envelope Kuvert
environment Umwelt
environmental impact *etwa:* Einfluß des Umweltgedankens; **impact** *auch:*
  Aufprall, Einschlag, Wirkung
Environmental Protection Agency Umweltschutzbehörde
environmentally friendly umweltfreundlich
equipment Ausrüstung, Anlage(n), Gerät(e)
era Ära, Zeitabschnitt
error Fehler, Irrtum
essential wesentlich
estate car Familienauto
even sogar, selbst
event Ereignis, Vorfall
eventual(ly) schließlich, letzten Endes
exasperated verärgert, wütend gemacht, aufgebracht
exclusive(ly) ausschließlich
exhaust Ausgangs…, Austritts…
exhaust gas Abgas(e)
exhaust port Auspuffkanal, Austrittsöffnung
exhaust valve Auspuffventil
exhibit Ausstellung, Ausstellungsstück
expatriate im Ausland lebender Staatsbürger
experience Erfahrung
experiences Erfahrungen; *sonst auch:* Erlebnisse
explorer Entdecker
extent *hier:* Größe, Außergewöhnliches
exterior das Äußere
external circuit Außenkreis, äußerer Stromkreis
extra muscle Zusatzkraft, -muskel

F
fairground Messegelände
fashion Weise
fast-growing schnellwachsend

fault Fehler, Defekt, Störung

fearsome gefahrvoll; *sonst auch:* schrecklich, grausam

feasible durchführbar

federal law Bundesgesetz

feed limit position Ende (*oder:* Endstellung) des Vorschubs

feed rate Vorschubgeschwindigkeit

feedwater Speisewasser

fell-walking Bergwandern; **fell** *auch:* Hügel

festive festlich, Fest...

festivities Festlichkeiten

field (Fach-)Gebiet

filthy unangenehm, schmutzig

final Schluss..., End...

financial means Finanzmittel

flange Flansch

flat (Etagen-)Wohnung

flat tyre *hier:* einen 'Platten'

flaw Fehler; *sonst auch:* Riss, Bruch

flawless fehlerfrei, fehlerlos

flooding Überfluten

flourishing gedeihend, blühend

fluctuation Schwankung

fluid Flüssigkeit

fly-wheel Schwungrad

fold Faltung

forecast Voraussage

fortuitous zufällig

founder Gründer

foundry Gießerei

four-seat aircraft Viersitzer-Flugzeug

four-stroke (diesel)-**engine** Viertakt(diesel)motor, Viertaktmotor

frame Ständer

freight Fracht

frozen (to freeze) gefroren

fuel Brennstoff, Treibstoff

fuel cell Brennstoffzelle; Stromquelle, in der durch elektrochemische Oxidation von Brennstoff mit Sauerstoff chemische Energie direkt in elektrische Energie umgewandelt wird

fuel injector Einspritzdüse

fuel Treibstoff, Brennstoff
fume unangenehmer Rauch, Dampf
furnace Industrieofen, Hochofen
furthest-advanced am weitesten fortgeschritten

G

gadget kleines Gerät, Spielzeug
gadgetry Apparate, technische Spielereien
gambit raffinierter Trick; *sonst auch:* Einleitung
gazebo Gebäude mit schönem Ausblick, Aussichtspunkt
gearbox Getriebe(kasten)
gears Zahnräder
gem Prachtstück, Edelstein
genuine(ly) echt, wirklich
giant Gigant
gland Stopfbuchse, Stoppbüchse
global sales Verkauf weltweit
goal Ziel
graduate degree Grad von einer Universität oder Fachhochschule (university or college)
gravity Gefälle; *sonst auch:* Schwerkraft, Schwere
grid Verbundnetz
growth Wachstum
grumblings Murren, Schimpferei
gudgeon pin Kolbenbolzen
gunning Aufdrehen, Aufheulen, Gasgeben

H

habits Gewohnheiten
handle bar grip Lenkstangengriff
hairy-chested halsbrecherisch, waghalsig, riskant
hand ratchet Handratsche, Handknarre; **ratchet** *auch:* Sperrklinke
hand-rolling Handroll…
handy handlich, praktisch
hazard Gefahr
heat-reflective wärmereflektierend
heavy industry Schwerindustrie
heavy oil Schweröl
heck Teufelszeug; *sonst auch:* Hölle

hefty wuchtig, gewaltig, 'saftig'
heyday Höhepunkt, Gipfel, Blütezeit
high marks gute Noten
high-volume world zu lärmige Welt, Welt voller Lärm
hold on bleib dran
hole Loch, Bohrung
host city gastgebende Stadt; **host** *auch:* Gastgeber
household removal Umzug mit dem (ganzen) Haushalt
household-control system Steuerungs- und Überwachungsanlage für den
  Haushalt
how-to guide Richtlinien für, Berater
hydrogen Wasserstoff
hype Trick, Finesse

I
icon Zeichen; sonst auch: Ikone, Heiligenbild
identification badge Abzeichen (*oder:* Schild) zur Identifikation, Zeichen zur
  Erkennung
illegible unleserlich
immediately sofort, unverzüglich
imminent drohend, bevorstehend
impeller Laufrad
impressed beeindruckt
impression Eindruck
improvement Verbesserung
in a course of während
in advance im voraus
in response to in Reaktion auf
in single file in einer Reihe
in stock auf Lager
in the event of im Falle, falls
inadequate unzureichend, ungenügend
inclusion Aufnahme, Einschluss
increasing ansteigend, wachsend
increasing(ly) immer mehr, wachsend
independent unabhängig
inferior minderwertig, zweitklassig
ink-jet printer Tintenstrahldrucker
innovation Erneuerung, Erfindung

innovations Neuerungen
inscrutable unergründlich
inspection hole Schauloch
instantaneous(ly) augenblicklich, sofort
insurance Versicherung
interim solution Zwischenlösung
interlock Verriegelung
internal combustion engine Verbrennungskraftmaschine
Internal Revenue Services Steuerbehörde
interstellar zwischen den Sternen befindlich
intrepid kühn, unerschrocken
introduction Einleitung, Einführung
inventor Erfinder
investigation Untersuchung, Nachforschung
itinerary Reiseziel

J
jacket Ummantelung, Hülle
jeep geländegängiges Fahrzeug, entstanden aus General-Purpose Vehicle
joint gemeinsam
junior engineer junger Ingenieur

K
key drawing Schlüsselplan, Hauptplan
kinks *hier etwa:* Ungereimtheiten; *sonst:* Knoten, Verzerrungen
knots: seamiles per hour; Knoten: 1,852 km/h

L
lack of youth das Fehlen des Neuen (*oder:* der Jugend)
landing gear Landegestell, Fahrwerk
language barrier Sprachbarriere, -schranke
lantern ring (split) Laternenring (zweiteilig, geschnitten)
last name Nachname
latter letztere
lavatory Toilette
law Gesetz
lawn Rasen
layer Schicht, Lage
layoff (vorübergehende) Entlassung, Freisetzung
leading role führende Rolle

leakage groove Lecknut
lean mager
lean-burn petrol engine Benzin-"Magermotor"
lecturer Dozent
legislation Gesetzgebung
lenient nachsichtig, milde
letter to the editor Leserbrief
lettering Buchstaben(auswahl)
lid Abdeckung, Deckel
lifting capacity Tragvermögen
light bulb Glühlampe
lighting Beleuchtung
limit switch Endschalter
liquid-crystal screen Bildschirm mit Flüssigkristall-Anzeige
lit (to light) erleuchtet, beleuchtet
literacy Fähigkeit zu lesen und zu schreiben
locking pins Sperringe, Spannringe
logs Holzblöcke
long-mooted schon lange diskutiert
low-speed langsamlaufend
lubricating property Schmiereigenschaft
lubricating system Schmieranlage, -system
lubrication Schmierung

M
M.S. Master of Science: Magister der Naturwissenschaften
machine tool Werkzeugmaschine
machining centre Bearbeitungszentrum
machining time Bearbeitungszeit, Grundzeit
maiden voyage Jungfernreise; **voyage** *allgemein:* längere Flug- oder
    Seereise
main bearing housing Kurbelwellen-Lagerstuhl
main motor Hauptmotor
main reason Hauptgrund
mains voltage Netzspannung
maintenance Wartung, Instandhaltung
major bedeutend; *auch:* wichtig, wichtigst, Haupt…
major savings wesentliche Einsparungen
mandatory vorgeschrieben, ein Muss

manoevring side Manövrierseite (Steuerstand)
manufacturer Farbikant
manufacturing Herstellungsbetrieb, Verarbeitungsunternehmen
marine diesel engine Schiffsdieselmoror
marvel Wunder(ding)
materials science Materialwissenschaft
mayor Bürgermeister
meagre kärglich, dürftig, mager, dürr
mean *hier:* Mittelwert
means of transport Transportmittel
measure *hier:*Vorkehrung
medium-size mittelgroß
medium-term thinking mittelfristiges Denken
member Mitglied
merchant vessel Handelsschiff
message Meldung, Nachricht
methodical(ly) methodisch, überlegt
mid-term Zwischen…, *sonst auch:* mittelfristig
mill Fabrik, Mühle
milling machine Fräsmaschine
minds on was das (ganze) Denken beeinflußt
mining equipment Bergbauausrüstung
misreadings falsches Ablesen
misunderstandings Missverständnisse
mothball Mottenkugel
motion Bewegung
move *hier:* Schritt
moving parts bewegliche Teile
mph (miles per hour) Meilen pro Stunde
must not *hier:* darf nicht

N
naval gun salute Salutschießen von Kriegsschiffen
necessary notwendig
neck bush Halsbuchse
neural networks neurale Netze; **neural** *sonst:* Nerven…
nitrogen oxides Stickstoffoxide
nitrogen Stickstoff
non-reversible nicht umsteuerbar

not at full stretch nicht voll ausgelastet
not caught on (to catch on) sich nicht durchgesetzt, nicht an Boden gewonnen
note Notiz(zettel)
notion Vorstellung, Begriff, Gedanke
novel neu(artig)
noxious giftig, Schadstoff…
nozzle Düse
number plate Nummernschild
nut (Schrauben-)Mutter

O
observation Beobachtung
obsolete veraltet, altmodisch
occupancy sensor Steuerungsgerät (*auch:* Sensor) für die Raumbesetzung
odd curse *etwa:* hin und wieder zu hörendes Fluchen
on a greenfield plant in einer Anlage im Grünen
on reaching beim (*oder:* mit) Erreichen
on the top oben auf
one-line diagram Übersichtsplan; *auch:* Hauptschaltplan
one-piece in einem Stück
operating pressure Betriebsdruck
operator 'Fräulein vom Amt'
operators *hier:* Betreiber
opinionated dogmatisch, schulmeisterlich, überheblich
opportunities Möglichkeiten, Gelegenheiten
orbit Umlaufbahn
order Bestellung, Auftrag *hier:* Größenordnung
ought to be sollten sein
output (abgegebene) Leistung
oven Herd; *auch:* Ofen
overhaul Überholung
oxygen Sauerstoff

P
p.m. (Lat.) post meridiem: after noon
p.s.i.g.: pounds per square inch gauged Pfund pro Quadratzoll gemessen
packing Packung
parachute Fallschirm
pattern Muster
peak (*or:* **top**) **demand** Höchstbedarf, Spitzenbedarf, Spitze

performance *hier:* Darstellung auf der Bühne; *sonst:* Leistung, Leistungsvermögen
period Zeit(raum), Periode
petrol Benzin; US: gasoline
petrol consumption Benzinverbrauch
petrol engine Ottomotor
petrol-burning mit Benzin arbeitend; *wörtlich:* Benzin verbrennend
Ph.D. Philosophy Doctor: Dr. der Philosophie
phenomenon Phänomen
piece of quartz Quarzstück
pipe branch Zweigleitung, Abzweigrohr
piston Kolben
plant Anlage, Fabrik
plaque Gedenktafel; *sonst auch:* Namensschild
plaything Spielzeug
plight Notlage, Zwangslage
plumber Klempner, Installateur
plumbing system Installationssystem (für Wasser, Gas usw.)
pollutants Schadstoffe, Verunreinigungen
polluter (Umwelt-)Verschmutzer, Umweltverseucher
Polytechnic Technische Universität
pope Papst
possessions Besitz(tümer)
pouch großer Beutel, Sack
power density Leistungsdichte
power station Kraftwerk
power tool Elektrowerkzeug
power-driven elektrisch betrieben
powerful leistungsstark
practitioner Praktizierende(r)
pre-ordained vorher eingestellt; **ordained** *sonst:* angeordnet, verfügt
precision engineering Präzisionstechnik
prediction Vorhersage, Prognose
preferred bevorzugt
preset vorher eingestellt
presidential address *hier:* Ansprache nach der Wahl zum Präsidenten
pressure switch Druckschalter
previous(ly) vorher, früher
prickly schwierig; *sonst auch:* dornig, stechend, stachelig

primarily hauptsächlich
priming Anfüllen
principle Prinzip
probable (-bly) wahrscheinlich
produce *hier:* Naturprodukte, Bodenprodukte
professional edge Vorteil (*oder:* Vorsprung) im Berufsleben; **edge** *sonst:* Schneide, Kante
proficiency Tüchtigkeit, Können
progress Fortschritt
prominent hervorstechend, führend
promising (viel)versprechend
proper(ly) ordnungsgemäß
prophets of doom Untergangspropheten; **doom** *auch:* Verhängnis, Schicksal
proponent Befürworter, Anhänger
proposal Plan, Vorschlag
propulsion system Antriebsanlage
prospective möglich(e)
proven (to prove) bewährt
public access area Räumlichkeit(en) für öffentlichen Zugang
publishing Verlagswesen
pump casing and cover Pumpengehäuse und Gehäusedeckel
pump shaft Pumpenwelle
pure rein, nur
push-button Druckknopf
putative vermeintlich, putativ
puzzled überrascht, verwirrt
pylon (freitragender) Mast

Q
quiet ruhig(laufend), geräuscharm

R
radio dish "Antennenschüssel"
rapid traverse Eilgang, Schnelldurchlauf
rated at *hier:* mit einer Nennspannung von, mit einer Nennleistung von
rating Bemessung, Auslegung
readily accessible leicht zugänglich
realm Bereich, Fachgebiet; *auch:* Königreich
reassuring beruhigend

recent(ly) kürzlich
rechargeable aufladbar
recommendation Empfehlung
recurring wiederkehrend, immer wieder auftretend
recycled wieder verwendet
red ensign rotes Zeichen; **ensign** *auch:* Flagge, (Rang-)Abzeichen
rediscovered wiederentdeckt
reduced verkleinert, reduziert
refrigerant Gefriermittel
refuelling (Wieder-)Auftanken, Nachtanken
refund Rückzahlung
reimbursement Entschädigung, Gutmachung, Rückvergütung
relationship Beziehung
relevant zutreffend, gültig
relief Erleichterung
relieved erleichtert, entspannt
rental fee Miet-, Leihgebühr
rented space vermietete Immobilien
repeat performance Wiederholungs-Vorführung
replacement Ersetzung, Ersatz
representative office Büro eines (Firmen-)Vertreters
required nötig, benötigt, erforderlich
research and development hub Zentrum für Forschung und Entwicklung; **hub**
   sonst auch: Angelpunkt, (Rad-)Nabe
research council Forschungsrat, Forschungskomitee
researcher Forscher
resident Bewohner
resort Erholungsort; *auch:* Zuflucht, Treffpunkt
responsible *hier:* ist zuzuschreiben; *sonst:* verantwortlich sein
result Ergebnis, Resultat
resulting sich (hieraus) ergebend
retail price Preis im Einzelhandel
retirement cake *hier:* Torte zur Pensionierung
rev/min revolutions per minute
revenues Einnahmen, Einkünfte; *sonst auch:* Finanzverwaltung
revival Wiederaufleben
revolution Umdrehung
reward(s) Gewinn; *sonst auch:* Belohnung, Anerkennung
rewarding lohnend, profitabel; *sonst auch:* dankbar

rigidity Festigkeit, Steifheit
rise Ansteigen, Vergrößerung
rocker arm Kipphebel
rocks Felsgestein
roller caster Achterbahnwagen
roof Dach
rough grob, rauh
rpm (*or: **rev/min**) **revolutions per minute** Umdrehungen pro Minute
rubber tire Gummireifen
rugged robust
rural areas ländliche Gebiete

S
sales department Vertriebsabteilung
sales potential Vertriebspotential
scaled-down verkleinert
scarce(ly) (sehr) selten
scavenging port Spülschlitz, Spülluftkanal
scenario Szenario, Plan; *auch:* (Film-)Drehbuch
schedule Plan, Aufstellung, Tabelle
score Menge, enorme Zahl
scrap lumber Holzabfall
screw Schraube
screwdriver Schraubenzieher
scruffy (Sl.) schmuddelig
section Abschnitt, Sektion
section leader Gruppenleiter
secure server *etwa:* Anschluß an sichere Bedieneinheit
seed crystal Impfkristall, Kristallkeim
self-contained unabhängig
senior älterer, Chef...
senior citizens ältere Bürger
series Serie, Reihe
serious(ly) ernst(haft)
servant Diener
service jobs Arbeiten im Dienstleistungsbetrieb
servicing Wartung; *manchmal auch:* Bedienung
shaft Schacht; *sonst auch:* Welle
shift Verlagerung, Verschiebung

ship's propulsion Schiffsantrieb
shipping company Reederei
short-listed auf der Auswahlliste, obenan
shortage Mangel, Bedarf, Knappheit
shower of sparks Funkenregen
shrine Heiligtum, Schrein
significance Bedeutung, Bedeutsamkeit
significant bedeutend, bedeutsam, wichtig
silicon (im Namen) Silizium
site Standort; *auch:* Baustelle
size Größe
slack schwach; *sonst auch:* schlaff, locker
sleeve Hülse; *sonst:* Ärmel
sleep mode "Schlafstellung"
slim and willowy rank und schlank
slim gering, dürftig; *auch:* schlank
small-loan Kleinkredit
smell Geruch
smooth weich, glatt
sober nüchtern
society Gesellschaft
solar energy Sonnenenergie
solenoid valve Magnetventil
solid core fester Kern
solid-state memory Festkörperspeicher
solidified carbon dioxide CO_2-Eis
solution Lösung
soot-blower Rußbläser
sophisticated hochentwickelt, 'raffiniert', äußerst leistungsfähig, fortgeschritten
sound richtig; *sonst auch:* gesund
source of power Energiequelle
space Platz, Raum, *hier:* Weltraum, Weltall
space travel Raumfahrt
spacious geräumig
spare *hier:* Reservereifen
spare motor Reservemotor
specification Bauvorschrift, Pflichtenheft, Spezifikation
speed *hier:* Drehzahl

spigot (Dreh-)Zapfen; *auch:* Zentriersatz
spot Stelle, Platz
spy Spion
square inch Quadratzoll
squeaky clean *hier etwa:* astrein
squirrel-cage induction motor Käfigläufermotor
stack Stapel, Schichtung
standby mode Bereitschaftsstellung
staple Haupterzeugnis, Stapelware
starting up Anlauf, Starten, Hochfahren
stated *hier:* bestimmt
stealth *hier:* Unauffälligkeit; *sonst:* Heimlichkeit
steam chest Ventilkasten
step-by-step stufenweise
strain Belastung, Spannung
stranger Fremder
striking auffallend, Eindruck machend
structure Konstruktion, Aufbau, Bauart, Bau(werk)
strut Strebe, Versteifung
stuffing box Stopfbüchse
sub *hier:* Verteil…, Unter…
subject Thema, Gegenstand
subsidiary Tochtergesellschaft
substrate Grundlage, Unterlage
subtitle Untertitel
subtitled mit Untertiteln versehen
succession Fortführung, Folgezeit
suction lift Saughöhe
suction pipe Saugleitung, Ansaugrohr
sufficient(ly) ausreichend
suggestion Meinung; *sonst auch:* Vorschlag
suitable (-bly) angemessen; *sonst auch:* passend, geeignet
suitable passend, geeignet
sulphur content Schwefelgehalt
sulphur Schwefel…
supply Zufluß; *sonst auch:* Lieferung, Versorgung
surface Oberfläche
surplus Überfluß, Überschuß
surprise Überraschung

survey Nachforschung, Überprüfung, statistische Erhebung, Untersuchung
swivelling Schwenken

T
table *hier:* Tabelle
tapeless ohne Band
task Aufgabe
tax return Steuererklärung
taxpayer Steuerzahler
telegraph pole Telegrafenmast; **pole** *auch:* Stange, Pfahl
telltale clicks verräterisches Klicken
temporary (-rily) zeitweise, vorübergehend
terms Voraussetzungen, Bedingungen
thatched roof Strohdach
theatre dressing room Theatergarderobe
throttle valve Drosselventil, Reglerventil
throttling Gas geben, Beschleunigen
thrust-block Drucklager; *sonst auch:* Querstück
time-lag relay Zeitrelais
took off (to take off) abhob
toolmaker's lathe (TM lathe) Drehmaschine für Werkzeugmacherei und
   Vorrichtungsbau
top official Chef an der Spitze
touch screen Kontaktbildschirm
toward(s) hin zum
toxic giftig, mit Schadstoffen versehen
trade fairs (Handels-)Messen
transition Übergang; *sonst auch:* Durchgang
transmission-line tower Leitungsmast für Stromübertragung
transverse girder Bindequerträger
truck (US) Last(kraft)wagen; GB: lorry
tube (*or:* **pipe**) Rohr, Leitung
tungsten lamp Glühlampe; **tungsten** *sonst:* Wolfram
turn of events Änderung der Gegebenheiten; *event. auch:* Ereignis,
   Vorfall
turquoise türkisgrün
turret lathe Revolverdrehmaschine
turret Revolver(kopf)
turret-type lathe Revolverdrehmaschine

two-wheeler Zweirad
tyre (US: tire) Autoreifen

U

unable nicht in der Lage, unfähig
unemployment lines Schlangen von Arbeitslosen
unhesitating(ly) ohne zu zögern
unprepared unvorbereitet
unworthy nicht vertretbar, unwürdig
upshot Fazit, Endergebnis
urban personal transport Personen-Stadttransport
urban renewal project Stadterneuerungsvorhaben
urgent dringend, dringlich, eilig
user Benutzer, Anwender

V

valley of the clueless Tal der Ahnungslosen
valuable wertvoll
value Wert, Bedeutung
van Lieferwagen
vapour Dampf…, Verdampfungs…
vehicle Fahrzeug
vent connection Entlüftungsanschluss
ventures Unternehmungen
veritable wirklich, echt
versatile vielseitig verwendbar
vessel Schiff; *sonst auch:* Gefäß, Behälter
vicinity Nähe
villainous-looking schurkisch aussehend
visible (-bly) sichtbar
voltage behaviour Spannungsverhalten
voltage level Spannungsniveau
voltage pulse Spannungsimpuls

W

wads of notes Banknoten-Bündel
was fairly described wurde gerechterweise (*auch:* gerecht, richtig) dargestellt
　oder: beschrieben
water cooling passage Kanal für Kühlwasserdurchlauf

water space Wasserraum
water vapour Wasserdampf
wave cycle Wellenzyklus
wave of unemployment Welle der Arbeitslosigkeit
wealth-building Reichtum schaffend
wearing property Laufeigenschaft, Verschleißeigenschaft
weatherman Meteorologe
weight Gewicht
well-maintained gut erhalten und gepflegt
wellnigh fast, so gut wie
white-collar job Büroberuf
widely used weit verbreitet, weit genutzt
winding Wicklung
wisecracks schlaue Bemerkungen, Witzeleien
with regard to hinsichtlich
witness Zeuge, Zeugnisaussage
work-related die Arbeit betreffend, zur Arbeit gehörend
worst of all am allerschlimmsten
worst-case für den schlimmsten Fall

Y
youth hostel Jugendherberge

Z
zero-emissions law Gesetz, betreffend schadstofflose Abgase

Verben:

to accelerate beschleunigen
to accept annehmen, akzeptieren
to acclimate sich akklimatisieren, gewöhnen an
to account for ausmachen, betragen
to accustom to sich gewöhnen an
to achieve erreichen, gelangen zu
to acquire (käuflich) erwerben
to activate betätigen
to add together zusammenschalten, -fügen
to adjust angleichen, justieren, einstellen, ausrichten

to admit zugeben, zugestehen

to adopt *hier:* verwenden; *sonst:* annnehmen, adoptieren, übernehmen

to advertise affluence Wohlhabenheit zur Schau stellen

to advertise anpreisen, propagieren, werben, inserieren

to advise unterrichten, mitteilen; sonst auch: (an)raten

to aim at (ab)zielen auf

to allow gestatten

to alter opinion Meinung ändern

to alter verändern

to announce ankündigen, verkünden

to answer the telephone Hörer abnehmen, Telefon beantworten

to anticipate sich darauf einstellen; *sonst:* erwarten

to appal erschrecken, entsetzen

to appeal to Anklang, Gefallen finden an

to appear erscheinen

to apply anwenden, verwenden

to arrive eintreffen, ankommen

to assimilate *hier:* eindringen; *sonst:* angleichen, anpassen, assimilieren

to assume annehmen, vermuten

to attend beiwohnen, teilhaben, besuchen

to attract anziehen

to avoid vermeiden

to award zuerkennen, gewinnen

to base on basieren auf

to be frisked durchsucht werden, 'gefilzt' werden

to be in for gut sein für, erstaunt sein über

to beam abgeben, strahlen

to behave sich verhalten

to bill itself sich selbst bezeichnen

to bill verkünden (zum Beispiel durch Plakate)

to blench zurückschrecken

to blend sich verschmelzen, vermischen

to boast sich rühmen; *auch:* prahlen

to bolster stärken, unterstützen; *sonst auch:* (aus)polstern, künstlich aufrecht erhalten

to bolt together zusammenschrauben

to boost erhöhen, steigern

to bring up to speed hochfahren (auf Nenndrehzahl)

to build bauen

to buoy by betreiben mittels
to burst into flames in Flammen aufgehen
to call on besuchen
to cancel aufgeben, streichen, absagen
to catch on Anklang finden, einschlagen; *sonst auch:* 'kapieren'
to cause veranlassen, bewirken; *sonst auch:* verursachen
to chip away abspanen, wegschneiden
to claim meinen, behaupten; *sonst auch:* Anspruch erheben
to coincide zusammentreffen, zusammenfallen, sich decken (mit)
to combine vereinigen, kombinieren
to come across *etwa:* bekannt vorkommen, schon einmal begegnet sein
to commence beginnen
to communicate mitteilen, übertragen
to compare vergleichen
to complain sich beschweren
to comprise umfassen
to confirm bestätigen, bekräftigen
to connect anschließen, schalten
to connect to each other gegenseitig verbinden
to connect to verbinden mit; *sonst auch:* anschließen an
to consider bedenken, erwägen
to consist of bestehen aus
to constitute bilden, darstellen
to construct bauen
to consume verbrauchen
to contain enthalten, aufnehmen, umfassen
to convert umbauen, umwandeln, verwandeln in
to cope with fertigwerden mit
to create herstellen, schaffen, kreieren
to cross the Channel den Kanal überqueren
to culminate in Spitze erreichen mit (oder: in)
to cut *hier:* verringern
to de-energize zum Abfall bringen, entregen
to deal with behandeln, zu tun haben mit
to decide (sich) entscheiden
to defy sich widersetzen, trotzen, die Stirn bieten
to deliver (ab)liefern, übergeben
to demand fordern, verlangen
to depict veranschaulichen, schildern

to deploy sich entfalten, einsetzen

to deposit ablagern, setzen

to design aufbauen, auslegen, konstruieren, entwerfen

to desire wünschen

to develop entwickeln

to devise sich ersinnen, ausdenken

to devote weihen, widmen

to disappear verschwinden

to discharge auslaufen; *sonst auch:* entladen

to disclose preisgeben, aufdecken

to discover entdecken

to disembark von Bord gehen, aussteigen

to dismantle abbauen, demontieren

to dissipate ableiten, abgeben; *sonst auch:* zerstreuen

to doom *hier:* aufgeben, verloren gehen lassen

to doubt Zweifel hegen

to draw anziehen, entnehmen; *sonst auch:* entziehen

to drill bohren

to drop fallen, niedergehen

to dwarf klein erscheinen lassen, in den Schatten stellen

to dwindle nachlassen, dahinschwinden

to earn erwerben, verdienen

to earn the keep sein Geld verdienen

to elapse verstreichen

to embark Passagiere und Fracht aufnehmen; *auch:* beginnen mit einem
   Vorhaben

to embrace erfassen, aufnehmen; *sonst auch:* umschließen, umarmen

to emerge kommen aus; *sonst auch:* auftauchen, erscheinen

to emit abgeben, ausstrahlen, emittieren

to emphasize hervorheben; *sonst auch:* betonen, Schwergewicht legen auf

to employ beschäftigen

to enable ermöglichen, in den Stand setzen

to encourage ermutigen, anregen

to energize erregen (Relais), betätigen, anreizen

to enjoy sich erfreuen

to ensure sichern, gewährleisten

to enter beginnen, einlaufen, eintreten in

to equip versehen, ausrüsten

to establish errichten, aufbauen

to estimate schätzen, vermuten
to evacuate entlüften
to expect erwarten
to explain erläutern, erklären
to exploit nutzen; *sonst auch:* ausbeuten
to explore erforschen, erkunden
to express sich ausdrücken
to extract entziehen, entnehmen
to fail fehlschlagen, danebengehen
to fasten befestigen
to feature als Besonderheit aufweisen
to feed *hier:* einleiten, einführen; *sonst auch:* speisen
to file the tax die Steuererklärung einreichen
to fill with dread mit großer Angst erfüllen; **dread** *auch:* Grauen
to fit einbauen, montieren, einsetzen, vorsehen
to fit into hineinpassen in
to fit the requirements den Anforderungen gerecht werden
to fit versehen, ausrüsten
to fizzle zum Misserfolg werden, danebengehen, schiefgehen
to fold falten, umbiegen
to force drücken, zwingen
to form sich bilden, formieren
to fuel betreiben, antreiben; *sonst auch:* Öl bunkern, auftanken
to generate hervorbringen; *sonst auch:* erzeugen
to get lost Orientierung verlieren, sich verlaufen
to go (*or:* **put**) **into service** in Dienst stellen
to go ahead weitermachen
to go astray vom Weg abkommen, das Ziel verfehlen
to grasp fassen; *sonst auch:* packen, ergreifen
to grouse meckern, nörgeln
to handle umgehen mit, handhaben
to harness nutzen, einspannen
to head for a first an die Spitze gelangen, erste(r) sein
to hurt oneself sich wehtun; *oder:* verletzen
to illuminate aufleuchten
to impress beeindrucken
to improve verbessern
to include einbeziehen, einschließen
to increase erhöhen, zunehmen, vergrößern, anwachsen

to indicate anzeigen; *sonst auch:* kennzeichnen
to insert einsetzen
to inspire inspirieren, veranlassen
to instigate anfachen; *sonst auch:* anstiften, aufhetzen
to intend beabsichtigen
to introduce einführen, vorstellen
to invent erfinden
to investigate untersuchen, nachspüren
to invite cordially herzlich einladen
to iron out ausbügeln
to join verbinden, verflechten, zusammenfügen
to keep an eye on beachten, Augenmerk richten auf
to launch starten; *sonst auch:* (Schiff) vom Stapel lassen
to lead führen
to leave on eingeschaltet (ver)lassen
to levy (Abgaben oder Gebühren) erheben
to lift the elbow a deal too much gern einen zuviel heben
to linger verweilen, zurückbleiben
to link verbinden
to load beladen
to locate *hier:* den Sitz feststellen, lokalisieren
to look after sich kümmern
to loom along aufragen über; *sonst auch:* von Bedeutung sein (bei, über)
to lose the hearing das Gehör verlieren
to lose weight Gewicht abnehmen
to lower herabsetzen
to lubricate schmieren
to machine bearbeiten (maschinell)
to machine together zusammen (d. h. gleichzeitig) maschinell bearbeiten
to maintain behaupten; *sonst auch:* beibehalten
to make a point es darauf anlegen
to make amends etwas gutmachen, kompensieren
to make up for wettmachen, ausgleichen
to measure messen, angeben, *hier:* Abmessungen aufweisen von
to monitor überwachen
to mount anbringen, aufbauen, befestigen, besteigen, montieren, sich widmen, vorsehen
to note feststellen, bemerken, meinen, angeben
to obtain erhalten, sich beschaffen

to occur vorkommen, auftreten
to offer bieten
to operate arbeiten, werden betrieben
to operate on arbeiten mittels, werden betrieben mit
to out-compete ausstechen
to outshine in den Schatten stellen, überstrahlen
to overcome fertigwerden (mit), bewältigen
to pack abdichten, verpacken, einbauen, einpacken
to pass through customs durch den Zoll gehen
to pay a visit Besuch abstatten
to pay duty Zoll zahlen
to perform ausführen, vornehmen
to persevere durchhalten, festhalten an
to persuade überreden, zureden
to piece together zusammensetzen
to point out darauf hinweisen, feststellen
to possess besitzen
to predict voraussagen, vorhersagen
to prefer bevorzugen
to prepare vorbereiten
to present darstellen
to press a button einen Knopf drücken
to press drücken
to prevent vermeiden, verhindern
to prime anfüllen
to proceed vorgehen
to proclaim ausrufen, verkünden
to produce erzeugen
to propel (an)treiben
to propose vorschlagen; *sonst auch:* planen
to prove beweisen, sich erweisen
to provide sichern, vorsehen; *sonst auch:* liefern
to publish veröffentlichen
to push out *hier:* unterdrücken
to put a call through einen Anruf durchstellen
to put it *hier:* es so ausdrücken
to put up aufbauen, einrichten
to quit aufgeben, verlassen
to raise the question die Frage erheben

to reach erreichen
to receive empfangen, erhalten
to reckon damit rechnen, halten für
to recognise (wieder)erkennen
to recommend empfehlen
to record aufnehmen, aufzeichnen
to redistribute umverteilen, neuverteilen
to reduce reduzieren, verringern
to refer to sich beziehen auf
to refund zurückerstatten, rückvergüten, gutmachen
to refuse sich weigern, verweigern
to regard betrachten
to reinvent neu erfinden
to release freigeben
to relegate zuschreiben; *sonst auch:* verbannen
to rely on beruhen auf, sich stützen auf, verlassen, bauen auf
to remain bleiben
to remark on sich äußern, bemerken über
to remove entfernen, herausnehmen
to render es schaffen, machen
to replace ersetzen
to report berichten
to request erfragen, veranlassen, bitten (um), ersuchen
to require benötigen, erfordern
to resort to zurückgreifen auf; *auch:* sich neu orientieren
to restore wieder in Ordnung bringen
to result from sich ergeben aus, resultieren aus
to retire in den Ruhestand treten
to return zurückkehren
to reverse umkehren
to revive wieder aufleben lassen; *sonst auch:* wiederbeleben
to roam around (*or:* **about**) durchstreifen, umherwandern (in)
to roar off davondonnern (*oder:* -röhren)
to rush sich beeilen, stürzen, stürmen, dahinjagen
to seal abschließen, abdichten
to set out sich dranmachen, beginnen
to share teilen
to shut down abstellen
to smooth glätten
to sound sich anhören, klingen, tönen

to span umfassen, umspannen
to speak volumes Bände sprechen
to spell out (mühsam) entziffern; *auch:* darlegen
to spend ausgeben, investieren
to squeeze unterbringen; *auch:* quetschen, drücken
to stake a claim Anspruch anmelden, Anspruch erheben
to stand apart für sich (selbst) betrachten
to state angeben, bestimmen
to stay alert wachsam bleiben, auf der Hut sein
to stretch sich dehnen, ausweiten
to strip entfernen, runterreißen
to stroll up bummeln, schlendern, (spazieren)gehen
to suffer a collaps einen Kollaps erleiden
to suggest hinweisen, hindeuten, vermuten lassen, bedeuten, vorschlagen
to suit passen, recht sein
to suit tastes and desires dem Geschmack und den Wünschen gerecht werden
to summon herbeirufen, herbestellen
to supersede ersetzen; *sonst auch:* abschaffen, beseitigen
to support verstärken, abstützen
to suppose annehmen, vermuten
to survive überleben, standhalten
to sweep hindurchfegen
to swivel in einschwenken
to swivel out zurückschwenken, ausschwenken
to take a toll Tribut fordern, arg mitnehmen
to take advantage die Vorteile nutzen
to tap entnehmen, (ab)zapfen
to tend dazu neigen
to the tune of in der Höhe von, man sage und schreibe
to toss (hinüber)schieben, werfen
to tout anpreisen, ausrufen, verkünden, aufdringliche Werbung betreiben
to transform into verwandeln in
to transmit übertragen
to treat behandeln
to trust vertrauen
to tune into hereinbekommen, sehen können
to turn down ablehnen
to turn into sich wandeln zu; *auch:* sich verwandeln in
to turn on and off ein- und ausschalten
to turn up erscheinen, auftauchen

to underscore unterstreichen, betonen
to unveil eröffnen, enthüllen
to update auf den neuesten Stand bringen
to usher hineinführen
to usher in einleiten
to vault *hier:* sich erheben, schwingen; *sonst auch:* springen
to vindcate Anspruch geltend machen
to wear a life jacket eine Schwimmweste tragen
to wear tragen
to weigh wiegen, wägen
to wire up verdrahten, anschließen
to wreck zerstören, zum Wrack machen
to yield einbringen, hervorbringen, ergeben; *sonst auch:* ernten
to zip *hier:* überholen; *sonst:* schwirren, rauschen

Redewendungen:

I could do with one ich könnte eine (Tasse Kaffee) gebrauchen
I used to know ich kannte, ich pflegte zu kennen
if my memory serves me right wenn ich mich recht erinnere
food for thought das gibt (aber) zu denken
for tabletop use auf den Tisch zu stellen
for the sake of form nur so, als Formsache
from top to bottom von oben bis unten
he became heated er regte sich auf
he is inclined er neigt dazu
is hitting the road ist auf der Straße anzutreffen; *oder:* zu finden
it looks set for es sieht aus wie
it must exact a toll es muß einen Tribut zollen; **to exact** *auch:* (Zahlung) einfordern, eintreiben; **toll** *auch:* (Brücken-)Zoll, (Hafen-)Gebühr
should not date *etwa:* es sollte auch weiterhin lesenswert sein; sollte zeitlich nicht begrenzt sein
the letter inside read im Brief stand geschrieben
they vied with each other (to vie) sie wetteiferten untereinander
things are coming along well *etwa:* bei uns läuft alles ganz gut
to die was cast die Würfel sind gefallen: *wörtlich:* der Würfel war gefallen
to knock the hell out of us uns die Hölle heiß machen
we've come to depend on von der wir nun alle abhängig sind
when the oil ran out wenn das Öl zur Neige gehen würde
without moving another inch ohne sich einen Zoll weiterzubewegen